THE THEORY
AND PRACTICE
OF BANK OWNED
LIFE INSURANCE

WARREN T. WAMBERG

T.W.O.
PUBLISHING

FASB Technical Bulletin No. 85-4, Accounting for Purchases of Life Insurance, © copyright by Financial Accounting Standards Board, 401 Merritt 7, P.O. Box 5116, Norwalk, Connecticut 06856-5116, U.S.A., is reprinted with permission.

Printed in the U.S.A.

10 9 8 7 6 5 4 3 2

ISBN: 0-9647664-0-X

PUBLISHING

T.W.O. Publishing
PO Box 66553 · Chicago, IL 60666-0553

ABOUT THE AUTHOR

Warren T. "Tom" Wamberg, CLU, is a Principal of the firm Clark/Bardes, Inc., which was founded in 1967. Mr. Wamberg's office is located in North Barrington, Illinois. The company designs and administers sophisticated life insurance plans for banks and commercial corporations.

The author's professional memberships include the American Compensation Association, American Society of Pension Actuaries, American Society of CLU & ChFC, and the Young Presidents' Organization. He also has served as the President of the 25 Million Dollar Forum, 1995 President Elect of the Association for Advanced Life Underwriting, and is on the Foundation Board of the University of the Americas in Mexico City.

ACKNOWLEDGMENTS

This book could not have been produced without the help of a lot of talented people. I am especially indebted to my friends and colleagues at Clark/Bardes. They were invaluable in rigorously reviewing and editing sections that pertain to their specialties within our company. The fact they did all this while never missing a deadline at the office is commendable.

My thanks to:

William Gallegos

Virginia Garrison, CPA

David Hart

Alison Hoffman

Frank Kelly, CCP

Dave Koenen

Carol Beatty Marsh

Andrea Pallo-DeLong

-Tom Wamberg, CLU
Barrington Hills, IL
October, 1995

TABLE OF CONTENTS

APPENDICES

INTRODUCTION

Bank owned life insurance (BOLI) has become a popular tool for financing the cost of employee benefit plan expenses. Introduced in 1987, BOLI today is a multi-billion dollar market. Many experts see the market doubling within the next few years.

Most BOLI buyers are buying this type of insurance for the first time. They need unbiased information. *The Theory and Practice of Bank Owned Life Insurance* offers a complete and candid overview of the subject, including all aspects of the purchase decision.

The book discusses how BOLI works and the reasons why banks increasingly use this product. In addition, it helps readers find their way through the maze of decisions that have to be made when purchasing a BOLI plan, ranging from financial performance analysis to impact on employees.

Bank owned life insurance presents a unique financial opportunity. *The Theory and Practice of Bank Owned Life Insurance* provides objective information that helps readers make sound decisions about what kind of plan best suits their organization. This book allows readers to understand the BOLI product in detail and design a smart, safe, and profitable plan for their institutions.

CHAPTER 1
AN OVERVIEW OF
BANK OWNED LIFE INSURANCE

Since 1987, banks have successfully profited with bank owned life insurance (BOLI) and in the past two years the product has gained wide acceptance within the banking community as a sound financial strategy. BOLI is insurance that is owned by the bank. The bank is also the beneficiary of the policies. Most banks have found that BOLI can provide after-tax returns 200 to 300 basis points higher than traditional bank investments with low risk.

The main reason banks use bank owned life insurance is to finance the cost of employee benefit plans. These expenses are a major overhead component for most banks. Any financing tool which can lower or stabilize this cost is of great value.

> Recent studies have suggested that benefit plan expenses will continue to increase at a much faster pace than the rate of increase in banks' interest income. Any plan that can control this increase makes good financial sense. BOLI is the most powerful tool available to help banks with this problem.

Banks gain two main advantages from using BOLI: the plan's yield is greater than that available from alternative investments, and the long-term nature of the program corresponds with the extended time horizon of benefit plan expenses.

HOW BOLI WORKS

A bank purchases life insurance covering a group of employees. The group can consist of all the institution's full-time employees or it can include only a select group, such as officers of assistant vice president rank and above.

The number of employees to be insured is determined based on two considerations: the total amount of money available to allocate to BOLI, and the bank's permissible level of benefit plan exposure calculated according to the Office of the Comptroller of the Currency (OCC).

OCC *BANKING CIRCULAR 249*

Banks may not simply purchase BOLI as an investment. The amount of coverage must conform with the bank's allowable benefit liabilities. (The OCC regulations are discussed in detail in Chapter 6.)

Once the number of employees to be insured has been selected and the size of the premium has been determined, the policies are issued to the bank. Most BOLI plans require only a one-time premium deposit.[1] The bank pays the premium and owns the entire cash value of the policies. The bank is also the beneficiary of the life insurance proceeds. Employees generally do not receive any of the insurance proceeds

---

[1] This is called "single premium life insurance" and is a modified endowment contract. Modified endowment contracts are explained in Chapter 4.

directly, nor do they pay any of the premium. The coverage is entirely separate from other insurance coverage provided by the bank, such as group term life insurance.

BOLI is not a new benefit for employees. It simply helps the bank pay for the benefits currently provided. Employees have reacted favorably to BOLI plans when they understand that BOLI allows their employer to finance its benefit plan obligations without requiring any payments from employees.

From a financial perspective, BOLI provides a bank with a high tax-free yield. The bank can pay premiums with funds derived from selling portfolio investments with lower tax-adjusted yields, such as U.S. Treasury securities and corporate bonds. (Chapter 4 illustrates how the yields from BOLI compare to these alternatives.)

Numerous studies demonstrate the relative advantages of BOLI measured over a period of decades. These analyses illustrate how insurance carriers can pass on competitive, tax-favored yields to banks.

A BOLI plan generates additional income as early as the first year it is put into effect and it continues producing additional income each year it is in force. The income comes from two sources: the growth of the asset (the cash value) and from the payment of death benefits to the bank when employees die.

From an accounting point of view, BOLI is subject to "FASB Technical Bulletin 85-4" (see Appendix B). This advisory was issued in 1985 in response to a request from the life insurance industry for an accounting standard covering life insurance owned by a corporation. Unlike accounting for some other financial instruments, the accounting treatment for BOLI is straightforward and noncontroversial.

Once the decision to purchase BOLI is made, the next step is to choose a life insurance carrier that has an acceptable performance record and financial credit rating. (Carrier selection is covered in Chapter 5.)

> BOLI plans have been promoted as a solution to the FAS 106 problem which requires a corporation to accrue for the cost of post-employment benefits other than pensions. BOLI is an acceptable funding device, but only if placed in a 501(c)(9) trust, commonly called a voluntary employee benefit association (VEBA).
>
> To qualify as a funded asset, BOLI has to be placed in the VEBA and must follow all VEBA trust rules which are in turn governed by the federal Employee Retirement Income Security Act (ERISA). The main deterrent to placing the BOLI in a VEBA trust is that proceeds must be dedicated exclusively to funding employee benefit plans. If the funds flow back to the corporation, they become taxable. To avoid this, most banks have elected to purchase BOLI at the bank level, where it is exempt from the requirement that policies be placed in a trust.

LEGAL ISSUES

A number of legal issues must be addressed in designing a BOLI plan. Life insurance regulations require that policies be filed and approved in the state of domicile of the bank. A multi-state banking company must adhere to the insurance laws of the state where its corporate headquarters is located.

State insurance laws are generally consistent, but the laws in the state of the bank's main location govern. In addition, a BOLI plan must follow the insurable interest laws of the host state. Such laws regulate the amount of coverage a bank can buy on any employee.

CONSULTANTS AND ADMINISTRATORS

A final consideration is choosing a consultant to assist in designing and implementing a plan and an administrator to manage it over its expected life span of more than 40 years. Naturally, the quality of consultants and administrators plays a large role in determining the ultimate profitability of the plan.

The BOLI design and implementation process is straight-forward. However, it can sometimes be clouded by hyperbole and confusion. Any buyer who follows the steps laid out in this book can avoid the pitfalls and will find the BOLI process easy to follow. By taking advantage of the advice contained herein, a buyer will be in a position to maximize the BOLI opportunity.

CHAPTER 2

BOLI AND BENEFIT COSTS

Employee benefits are a significant expense item in bank compensation programs, comprising 20 to 30 percent or more of all compensation costs. Employee compensation is generally the second largest expense item for financial institutions. Only the cost of funds is a greater expense.

> Financial organizations, like all businesses, are concerned with the rising cost of employee benefits. BOLI allows them to design a plan that will offset a portion of employee benefit expenses and enhance financial performance.

This chapter explains the calculations required to determine a bank's benefit costs and therefore the amount of BOLI a bank may buy.

Generally, banks are not allowed to invest in life insurance products. Under specific circumstances banks may purchase life insurance to offset employee expense obligations. Regulators who oversee the safe and sound management of financial institutions have formulated guidelines for implementing BOLI plans. The Office of the Comptroller of the Currency (OCC) regulates allowable transactions for nationally chartered banks. The Office of Thrift Supervision (OTS) regulates savings associations. State banking agencies regulate state-chartered banks which are also under the jurisdiction of the Federal Reserve System or the Federal Deposit Insurance Corporation (FDIC). Each of these regulatory agencies limits the amount of life insurance a financial institution may purchase to an amount corresponding with benefit costs. In addition, the amount purchased may not exceed a certain percentage of a bank's capital and legal lending limits.

EMPLOYEE BENEFIT EXPENSES AND BOLI

For virtually every employee, benefits are a significant portion of overall compensation. Human resources managers regularly evaluate competitive practices and products in the marketplace to ensure their programs provide benefits that are meaningful, competitive, reasonable and cost-efficient. When financial institutions provide benefits for their employees, an obligation is created. Regulators have recognized the long-term cost of employee benefits by allowing financial institutions to utilize BOLI plans to offset their continuing liability. It is this continuing benefit liability that establishes the maximum limits for BOLI plan purchases by each financial institution. Regulators want to ensure that banks can meet benefit obligations without jeopardizing depositors or shareholders.

OCC *Banking Circular 249* defines the circumstances under which national banks may own life insurance. OTS and state regulations closely parallel OCC rules. The main principle of *Banking Circular 249* is clear:

> A bank may, therefore, purchase insurance on a group of persons and continue to hold the insurance as long as it has any liability under the associated compensation or benefit plan.

18

It is a common interpretation of *Banking Circular 249* that expenses associated with funded benefits are included in determining overall benefit expense obligations. Nonqualified benefit expenses are also included in calculating expense obligations. Employee benefit plans that are typically included in the calculation of expense obligations for BOLI are:

- Post-Retirement Medical
- Life Insurance
- Retirement Plan Expense — Qualified and Nonqualified

Calculating benefit expenses and obligations for BOLI is relatively straightforward. The maximum amount of coverage that may be purchased is determined according to the following procedure:

1. For each employee, the current benefit cost is calculated and then projected over the employee's working career.

2. The present value of the total employee benefit cost is then calculated for the date of BOLI plan implementation.

3. The total present value benefit cost for all employees is determined. This establishes the BOLI plan maximum limitations.

Since the bank in our example on page 20 has 1,000 employees, the maximum amount of insurance the bank can hold in its BOLI plan (on a present value basis) is $30,453 times 1,000 or $30,453,000. This means the total benefit from the 1,000 insurance policies cannot exceed a present value of $30,453,000. The limit corresponds to the bank's maximum employee benefit obligation of $30,453,000. Purchasing insurance beyond the benefit obligation is considered an investment and is not allowed.

PRESENT VALUE BENEFIT COST FOR ONE SAMPLE INDIVIDUAL

MALE, AGE 39

	Current Annual Cost	Inflation Factor	Future Value of Annual Benefit Cost at Age 65	Present Value of Annual Benefit Costs at 4%
Group Term Life	$190	5%	$676	$5,826
Pension Costs	$400	5%	$1,422	$12,265
Post-Retirement Medical	$320	7%	$1,858	$12,362
Total Net Present Value Cost				$30,453

Individual policies in a BOLI plan do not have to match the level of liability of each covered person. For example, a group of 200 employees can be insured to offset the costs associated with all 1,000 employees. This is called aggregate funding, as opposed to specific funding. In many cases, a bank will only insure its officers, purchasing enough BOLI to offset the benefit costs for all employees. It is more efficient to insure a smaller group of employees and policy administration is simpler.

It is not required that BOLI plan assets be segregated. They may be commingled with other bank assets. Appreciation in BOLI cash value is used to offset the cost of benefit expenses or obligations and is tax-free. Insurance proceeds are also nontaxable income to the bank.

Banks, their consultants, or actuaries use census information for each employee — age, sex, compensation, and other information — to calculate the present value cost of benefit expenses or obligations. In turn, the present value cost of benefit expenses determines the face amount of each policy. Insurance carriers also require adherence to insurable interest rules[1] which are aimed at preventing banks from collecting "profit" when an employee dies.

---

[1] *Insurable Interest:*

A bank must have an insurable interest to purchase life insurance on an employee. An explanation of insurable interest is covered, in detail, on page 25.

The concept that banks stand to profit from employee deaths is a frequent misconception about BOLI plans. Except in extraordinary circumstances, such as the death of large numbers of covered employees soon after plan implementation, banks do not profit from the death of any employee in a BOLI plan.

Banks can only purchase life insurance equal to the present value limits of their employee benefit expenses and are not allowed to speculate or over-insure any employee.

Insurance carriers limit the amount of insurance they will place on any single person based on insurable interest. The owner of the policy, a bank, must have an interest in the life of the insured, an employee. In most states, the net death benefits from a policy cannot be greater than the loss to a bank when an employee dies.

Sometimes when employees die early in a BOLI plan, a bank may appear to profit. But the plan is designed to finance a long-term obligation. In calculating that obligation, an expected mortality pattern for the total employee group is factored in.

INSURABLE INTEREST — THE GUIDELINES

In order for a bank to insure an employee, it must have an insurable interest.[2] *(See footnote on page 24.)* Insurable interest laws in this country were first enacted at the beginning of the 20th Century. Centuries ago in England, it was common to take bets or place insurance on the life of a sick person. Bettors would try to predict when a person would die. In the U.S., many states passed insurable interest laws outlawing this morbid practice.

From the early part of this century until the mid-1980s, the insurable interest laws were adequate for business practices.

THE BALANCE OF BOLI

Out of Balance without BOLI

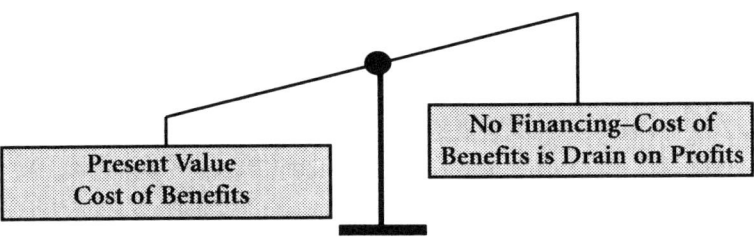

In Balance with BOLI

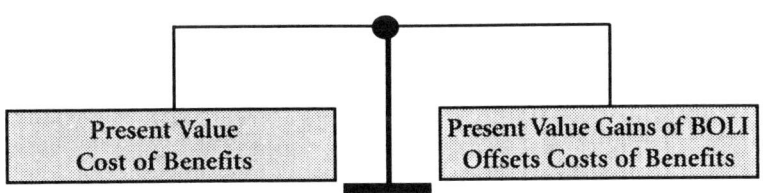

BOLI plans do not change any of the bank's employee benefits. BOLI is simply a financial tool used to offset the cost of these plans.

However, in the mid-1980s, a number of major companies set up Corporate Owned Life Insurance plans, the first time that large numbers of employees were insured with their employers as beneficiaries.

Prior to 1985, most corporations insured only their top executives for the benefit of the company. This concept of key-person insurance is well founded in the law and has been used extensively.

However, when corporations began to insure large groups or all employees, not just key persons, it raised the question of whether they were gambling on the probability of death of their employees, thereby running afoul of insurable interest laws. Of course, they were not really doing so, because the basic idea behind buying Corporate Owned Life Insurance is to offset the cost of death, not to make a profit.

The concept of insurable interest holds that a beneficiary, whether a family member or an employer, must have a pecuniary (monetary) loss that corresponds with the amount of life insurance carried on an insured person's life. The potential for a financial loss on one person's death creates an insurable interest for another person or entity that would suffer the loss.

---

[2]For more detailed information, see:

> Greider, Janice E., et al. *Law and the Life Insurance Contract.* Homewood, Illinois: Richard D. Irwin, Inc. 1984

> Black, Kenneth and Skipper, Harold. *Life Insurance.* Englewood Cliffs, New Jersey: Prentice Hall, Inc. 1987

Any individual may potentially be insured by a number of people or entities. For example, family members who are financially dependent on a bread winner have an insurable interest. The bread winner's employer would also suffer a loss if the employee died. Therefore, the employer also has an insurable interest, although the amount may be different.

In employer/employee situations, there are well established procedures for determining the amount of insurable interest. The first step is to consider the insurable interest laws covering the employer that is buying the coverage. Insurance is under the jurisdiction of the states. Employers with employees in many states will normally be governed by the laws of the state in which they have their corporate headquarters.

A number of states have enacted new insurable interest laws in response to employers who wish to insure large groups of employees. These states are:

Arizona	Maryland
Arkansas	Michigan
California	Minnesota
Delaware	Missouri
Georgia	New Jersey
Illinois	North Carolina
Kansas	Oklahoma
Maine	Virginia

These new laws allow corporations to insure all employees and, in some cases, retirees for the benefit of the corporation. The amount of coverage that may be purchased is determined by the employer's employee benefit plan expenses, similar to the standard applied in *Banking Circular 249*.

Banking Circular 249 varies from the states' approach in the types of benefits used in determining an allowable transaction. The types of benefits mentioned in the circular are:

- Post-retirement medical benefits
- Life insurance benefits
- Nonqualified retirement plan benefits

Most of the states listed above allow a corporation to insure an employee for an amount equal to the present value cost of the corporation's ERISA welfare benefit plans. ERISA welfare benefit plans include all non-retirement benefit programs. The cost is calculated identically to the example presented on page 19.

The cost of benefits and the amount of insurance which can be purchased is determined on an *aggregate* basis. This means the total amount of insurance cannot exceed the total amount of benefit costs for all employees. The amount of insurance on any individual employee can be more or less than the cost for that particular employee as long as the present value gain of the insurance on all employees does not exceed the benefit cost for the overall employee population. This method is known as the welfare benefit projection method.

In states without new insurable interest laws, corporations can insure non-key employees by completing a pecuniary loss calculation. This calculation is somewhat subjective and should be done by a firm that is knowledgeable about insurable interest regulations.

Under a pecuniary loss or pecuniary interest approach, a corporation must define the amount of loss it stands to suffer on the death of an employee. This loss is determined by the costs an employer would incur for benefits when an employee dies, plus any loss of productivity. Most corporations have group term life plans which have an experience rated feature. Under an experience rated plan, a corporation has a premium structure tied to the amount of its claims. For example, assume a typical employee has a salary of $25,000 and a group term life benefit of twice salary, or $50,000. If the employee were to die, the corporation would be charged the amount of the claim plus the carrier's expense margin, normally four percent. Therefore, the company's cost should be $52,000.

In addition, the employer would have other costs associated with the death of the employee, such as hiring and retraining costs. Studies show these costs average from two to 12 times a person's salary. Conservatively, the employer would incur another $50,000 in such costs upon the employee's death.

In addition, there is a factor for salary growth. Normally, a corporation would only insure an employee one time. Therefore, it is reasonable to add another two times salary to cover pay increases.

Total potential costs add up as follows:

Average Employee Salary	$ 25,000
Employer's Cost at Death	
• Group Term Life (two times salary plus 4% for carrier's expense margin)	$ 52,000
• Hiring & Retraining (two times salary)	$ 50,000
• Survivor Benefits	$ 25,000
• Salary Inflation (two times salary)	$ 50,000
TOTAL =	$202,000

Either the employee benefit plan expense method or the pecuniary loss method is useful to satisfy state statutes and insurance carrier requirements. The calculations performed under *Banking Circular 249* and the insurable interest determination reinforce each other, providing a strong undergirding for BOLI face amounts.

A final point is worth mentioning. A bank only needs an insurable interest in an employee at the time the coverage is written. If the employee leaves, coverage can remain in force. The law recognizes that if insurance were required to be canceled at termination of employment, it would not mature as a death benefit and would be paid as a cash surrender. If a policy is surrendered, the cash value in excess of premiums is taxable as ordinary income. State laws are designed to avoid forcing employers, or individuals for that matter, to cancel insurance and pay tax. Therefore, coverage is allowed to remain in force until death of the insured.

CHAPTER 3

THE VARIETY
OF BOLI PRODUCTS

To those buying insurance, the number of products can seem endless. Choosing the best one is a daunting task. However, armed with an understanding of life insurance, and how various products are built, banks will easily be able to select the products that best suit their needs.

> Broadly, life insurance products can be categorized as either term or permanent. Term life insurance provides coverage for a limited period of time and develops little or no cash value. In contrast, permanent life insurance provides coverage over the entire lifetime of the insured and generates cash value while the insured is alive. BOLI plans are always permanent life insurance because the cash value growth associated with this insurance is a key source of the earnings offered by the program.

Cash value generated by permanent life insurance represents an asset for a policy owner, such as a bank, and a liability for an insurance company. To back up that liability, the insurance company sets up a policy reserve. The method for determining the minimum policy reserve is regulated by state insurance departments, although an insurance company may strengthen its reserve position above the minimum at its discretion.

These reserve assets are held either in an insurance company's general account or in one or more separate accounts. Products whose supporting assets reside in an insurance company's general account are called portfolio products. Products whose supporting assets are held in separate accounts are referred to as variable products.

Whether portfolio or variable, a permanent life insurance product comes in one of four basic policy types, or chassis. The difference among them is a matter of mechanics, not value, which is determined by an insurance company's pricing and reflected in the levels of cash value and death benefits provided.

GENERAL ACCOUNT AND SEPARATE ACCOUNT PRODUCTS

Traditionally, insurance companies have sold products that promise fixed-dollar benefit payments when covered events occur, such as the death of an insured person. Assets that back these liabilities are held in an insurance company's general account.

Many of today's sophisticated insurance buyers are not satisfied with fixed-dollar benefits. They are keenly aware of the attractive returns available from the securities markets. The bull markets of the 1980s and the early 1990s fed the demand for products that would allow insurance buyers to capture market gains.

Responding to that need, many insurance companies now offer products whose benefit levels vary according to the market value of underlying assets. Insurance companies hold these assets in separate accounts from their general accounts. The products supported by these assets are referred to as separate account products.

General and separate account products also differ in the extent of liability of the insurance company. In addition to the fixed-dollar benefit liabilities, the general account is also charged with the general liabilities of the insurance company. In contrast, assets of separate accounts cannot be charged with liabilities that arise from other company business. Thus, a separate account product provides a BOLI buyer a greater degree of credit risk protection than a general account product.

PRODUCT CHASSIS

Permanent life insurance products are offered in one of four chassis: traditional whole life, interest-sensitive whole life, universal life, and variable life insurance.

TRADITIONAL WHOLE LIFE

Traditional whole life, as its name suggests, is the oldest form of permanent life insurance and accounted for most permanent life insurance sales until the 1980s. Beginning in the late 1970s, when interest rates were rising rapidly, the insurance industry suffered severe disintermediation by policy owners. To stem this tide, the industry developed products that responded more quickly and more visibly to interest rate movements. These products took the form of either interest-sensitive whole life or universal life.

When a policy owner buys a traditional whole life policy, he or she buys a schedule of guaranteed minimum cash value and death benefits. The guaranteed policy values are calculated based on a four percent interest rate and the 1980

Commissioners Standard Ordinary (CSO) Mortality Table. An insurance company makes an additional promise — though not a guarantee — to pay any excess profits back to the policy owner in the form of dividends. The sources of excess profits may be:

- Better-than-planned mortality experience
- Better-than-planned investment return
- Better-than-planned expense outlays

Forms of Dividends

An insurance company normally reviews its dividend formula once or twice a year. At each anniversary, the company calculates the dividend payable on the policy based on the prevailing dividend formula. A policy owner may take the dividend in a number of forms:

- Cash
- Paid-up life insurance
- One-year term insurance

Under the paid-up life insurance option, the dividend is used to purchase additional permanent life insurance coverage that requires no further premium payments and permanently increases the policy owner's coverage. With the one-year term insurance option, the dividend is used to purchase coverage that lasts only one year. This represents a temporary increase in coverage greater than that which could be purchased under the paid-up life insurance option.

Nonforfeiture Options

A policy owner must pay the scheduled premium when it is due to keep the traditional whole life policy in force. If the premium is not paid during a grace period of 30 to 60 days, the policy will lapse unless the owner has signed up for an automatic premium loan or partial surrender of paid-up life insurance coverage. Under the automatic premium loan election, a policy owner authorizes an insurance company to use the policy's available cash value as collateral to secure a loan from the insurance company that is used to pay the scheduled premium. Loan interest is also charged to the cash value. When the cash value can no longer cover accumulated premium loans and interest, the policy lapses. The policy owner will then have no further coverage.

If partial surrender of paid-up insurance is elected, an insurance company will surrender enough units of paid-up insurance coverage at the end of the grace period to pay for the scheduled premium. The partial surrender decreases the net coverage amount. Since the guaranteed cash value of the base policy cannot be surrendered in part, the policy will lapse when all paid-up insurance has been depleted. At that time, the policy owner still has the base policy's guaranteed cash value which can be disposed of as cash, reduced paid-up insurance or extended term insurance.

Under the reduced paid-up insurance option, the guaranteed cash value is applied toward the purchase of single-premium permanent life insurance. The coverage is reduced but will last for the remaining lifetime of the insured. Under the extended term insurance option, the guaranteed cash value is used to buy term insurance with the same coverage amount as the base policy. The duration of coverage is a function of the amount of guaranteed cash value, face amount, and age of the insured.

The previous examples are referred to as standard non-forfeiture options and are offered by almost every insurance company. Some insurance companies may offer additional options.

Paid-up Insurance Rider

To enhance policy performance, most insurance companies offer a paid-up insurance rider. It operates very much like a paid-up life insurance dividend option. The commission payable on the rider is much lower than that which is payable on the base policy itself. By combining sufficient units of paid-up insurance rider with the base policy, the policy owner can reduce the effective commission rate and thereby enhance returns on the insurance policy.

INTEREST-SENSITIVE WHOLE LIFE

Traditional whole life products are sometimes referred to as "bundled" products. Because insurance companies perform dividend calculations internally and report the results to policy owners as single sums, there is no way owners can determine expense levels, investment returns, and the effective charges made for mortality. Since they have no information on rates of return, they can easily be tempted to surrender the policy during a period of rising interest rates, as happened during the late 1970s and early 1980s.

In an attempt to retain business during periods of rising interest rates, the insurance industry developed the interest-sensitive whole life policy, also known as excess interest whole life. With this policy, a buyer receives a guaranteed, or tabular, schedule of minimum cash values and death benefits which are based on a four percent interest rate and 1980 CSO Mortality Table, just like traditional whole life policies. The distinguishing trait of the interest sensitive policy is the creation of a paper account called an accumulation account used to determine current, as opposed to guaranteed, cash values.

The accumulation account begins with a value of zero at issue. When the first premium is paid, front-end charges are deducted and the balance is credited to the account. At the beginning of each policy month, mortality charges and other charges specified in the contract, such as the policy administration fee, are deducted from the account. At the end of each policy month, interest is credited on the account balance. The interest rate is declared by an insurance company at the beginning of each policy year and is usually applicable for the entire policy year even though the insurance company may change the rate credited to new policies. The account value is updated on a monthly basis.

At any given time, a policy owner's cash value is equal to the accumulation account balance less any back-end surrender charges. The surrender charge is typically based on a decreasing schedule so that after ten years it disappears. The surrender charge is designed to allow the insurance company to recoup a portion or all of the first year's unrecovered expenses. The current cash value is never less than the tabular cash value specified in the contract.

This type of product adds a variable interest component to the return provided by a permanent life insurance policy. In this regard, interest-sensitive whole life is markedly different from traditional whole life. However, just like traditional whole life, premiums must be paid when due to keep the policy in force unless the policy owner has elected to use an automatic premium loan or a premium vanish.

Automatic Premium Loan and Premium Vanish

Non-forfeiture options are available with interest-sensitive whole life like those offered with traditional whole life insurance. The automatic premium loan feature is the same under both forms of insurance.

Under the premium vanish option, an insurance company projects the current cash value out to age 100, assuming no future premiums are paid. A comparison is made at each future policy anniversary between the projected current cash value and the tabular cash value. As long as the projected current cash value is equal to or greater than the tabular cash value at every future policy anniversary, a policy owner may suspend premium payment for the upcoming policy year. This process is repeated at every policy anniversary to determine whether the owner may continue to suspend premium payment. Insurance companies offer several variations of this option.

UNIVERSAL LIFE

Universal life was first introduced in 1979. It was developed to provide policy owners a flexible product that can easily be restructured to meet changing insurance needs. Universal Life now accounts for a significant portion of in-force permanent life insurance.

Under a universal life policy, an insurance company maintains an accumulation account for determining cash value. Universal life has a flexible premium, meaning that a policy owner may pay premiums at will, within certain limits. Premiums are credited to the accumulation account after deducting for premium loads. Mortality charges and other expenses are deducted from the account at the beginning of each policy month and interest is credited at the end of each policy month. The cash value is equal to the accumulation account balance less any applicable surrender charge.

Insurance companies do not guarantee a schedule of minimum cash values or death benefits under universal life. Instead, they guarantee that they will neither charge more than the 1980 CSO Mortality Table in mortality charges nor credit less than four percent interest in calculating the accumulation account balance. Further, expense loads charged to the account cannot exceed those allowed under state insurance regulations. Insurance companies must disclose interest rates and expenses.

A universal life insurance policy will stay in force as long as the accumulation account balance is sufficient at the beginning of each policy month to pay a mortality charge and other expenses. An insurance company sends a policy owner a notice of impending lapse if there is an insufficient balance in the account. At the end of each policy year, an insurer sends a statement disclosing charges and credits made to the accumulation account over the preceding twelve months.

An owner of a universal life policy need not follow any schedule of premium payment as long as there is sufficient value in the owner's account to pay the next month's mortality charge and other expenses. However, there are limits to premium flexibility.

An insurance company typically requires policy owners to make a minimum payment before it will issue the policy. Some insurance companies also require payment of small premiums for a specified period of time, such as three to five years, to keep a policy in force.

Moreover, policy owners cannot pay premiums exceeding those allowed under Section 7702 of the Internal Revenue Code *(see Appendix F)*. If they exceed these limits, contracts will not qualify as life insurance and policy owners will lose all tax advantages associated with life insurance.

With universal life, the default non-forfeiture option is extended term insurance. A policy owner may trigger this option just by not paying premiums. Alternatively, the owner may elect a cash distribution or reduced paid-up insurance.

VARIABLE LIFE INSURANCE

Variable life insurance was introduced in the United States in 1976 after gaining acceptance in Europe. Variable life allows policy owners to invest in a variety of asset funds, potentially offsetting the adverse effects of inflation on life insurance policy values. Variable life investment options now include:

- Money market funds
- Bond funds
- High yield bond funds
- Common stock funds
- Growth stock funds
- Income funds
- Global equity funds
- Global bond funds
- Real estate funds
- Precious metal funds
- Asset allocation funds

Common stocks are viewed as an effective long-run hedge against inflation. However, the short-run returns of stock are volatile. Banks generally may not invest in stocks, putting the equity options in variable life off limits to them. For that reason, a variety of investments are available through variable life suitable for buyers with different regulatory circumstances and levels of risk tolerance.

In a variable life insurance policy, premiums minus expense loads and mortality charges are placed in one or more investment subaccounts, as directed by a policy owner, within certain limits. The death benefit and the cash value of a policy vary according to investment results or, put another way, the fair market value of the subaccounts. Typically, the death benefit does not fall below a guaranteed minimum. However, there is no minimum guarantee for the cash value. Therefore, variable life insurance passes all investment risk from an insurance company to a policy owner. The insurance company retains the expense and mortality risk.

In addition to the restrictions of state insurance laws and regulations, variable life insurance is subject to regulation by the Securities and Exchange Commission and must adhere to federal securities laws, including The Securities Act of 1933, The Securities Exchange Act of 1934, and The Investment Company Act of 1940.

The Securities Act of 1933 and Securities Exchange Act of 1934

The Securities Act of 1933 mandates registration requirements for new securities. These requirements are designed to provide investors with the information they need to make intelligent decisions about securities purchases. Variable life investments are treated as securities under the law. As issuer of the security, an insurance company must file a registration statement with the SEC and prepare a prospectus for distribution to prospective investors. This prospectus must disclose the nature of the insurance company's business, the use to which premiums will be put, financial information about the insurance company, fees and expenses to be charged under the variable life insurance policy, and the policy owner's rights.

The Securities Exchange Act of 1934 regulates the secondary securities market. Under this law, a firm that distributes variable life insurance must register as a broker-dealer. All broker-dealers and persons associated with the sale of variable life insurance must register with the National Association of Securities Dealers and pass a securities examination. In addition, the 1934 Act requires periodic disclosure by insurance companies to policy owners.

The Investment Company Act of 1940

Under the Investment Company Act of 1940, a variable life insurance separate account, composed of various investment subaccounts, and corresponding investment funds must register as investment companies. Typically, the separate account is registered as a unit investment trust. Investment funds are registered as open-end diversified management investment companies. The 1940 act also regulates the management and operation of these investment companies, sets maximum sales charges, and requires the investment companies to distribute periodic financial reports.

Private Placement Variable Life Insurance

In recent years, a few insurance companies have begun to offer a new type of variable life insurance known as private placement variable life insurance. Private placement variable life insurance is exempt from registration requirements under Rule 506, part of Regulation D of the Securities Act of 1933. Under the act, an insurance company must ensure that a prospective policy owner is an accredited investor or an unaccredited investor who "...has such knowledge and experience in financial and business matters that he is capable of evaluating the merits and risks of the prospective investment."

Accredited investors include institutional investors, such as banks and mutual funds, and wealthy individuals. An insurance company can sell to no more than 35 unaccredited purchasers who meet the rule's criteria. In addition, Rule 506 prohibits insurance companies from publicly marketing private placement products.

Private placement variable life insurance is designed mainly for large institutional buyers. Loads, charges and policy provisions are negotiated between buyers and insurance companies within the constraints of state insurance regulations.

An insurance company usually will allow buyers to select one or more outside investment managers in place of the company or any of its subsidiaries to manage all or part of a policy's assets. Insurance companies normally will sell private placement variable life insurance and permit outside investment managers only for large accounts above a minimum case size (i.e., $1,000,000 of premium).

AN ALTERNATIVE HYBRID PRODUCT: PROTECTED EQUITY PLAN® (PEP)

The advantage of variable life insurance is its ability to provide banks greater long-term return potential compared to portfolio life insurance. This reflects the option offered by variable life to select riskier assets, such as high-yield bonds.

The disadvantage of variable life insurance is the greater potential for short-term volatility of returns. While portfolio life insurance protects the buyer from capital loss, variable life insurance provides no such protection. Thus, if financial markets are performing poorly, a bank may have to mark its assets to market and report a loss on its income statement. This is something all financial institutions want to avoid. Yet, if it avoided all risk, a bank would sacrifice opportunities to earn higher returns.

In order to provide a higher yield than a portfolio policy and to avoid the market swings of a variable product, a hybrid product has been developed called the Protected Equity Plan® (PEP). PEP, a trademarked product, provides a buyer a potential return equal to a certain percentage, called the participation rate, of the increase in the *Standard and Poor's 500 Stock Price Index* for the year. At a minimum, the buyer is guaranteed a return at least equal to a predetermined floor always greater than zero, even if the stock market plunges. On the upside, there is a cap on the buyer's potential return, regardless of how well the stock market performs. As the name suggests, a bank enjoys capital protection with PEP, while giving itself an opportunity to gain from a rising stock market.

How does PEP compare with portfolio life insurance and variable life insurance? The table on the following page demonstrates the hypothetical performance over the last 20 years if PEP had been available. An average of the top life insurance companies rated by dividend performance was used to determine the historical interest rate of the portfolio life insurance contracts.

The returns and volatility exhibited by PEP would have fallen between portfolio life insurance and variable life insurance. PEP would have earned a positive return every year, so banks would never have had to write down assets or report losses in their income statements. PEP would have accomplished this while offering a higher return than portfolio life insurance. For most investors, this would have provided the best of both worlds.

INSURANCE COMPANY INVESTMENT STRATEGIES

In order to be able to honor their obligations to policy owners, insurance companies structure their investment portfolios to produce cash flows that closely mirror their liabilities. The structure of their liabilities reflects the types of insurance products they sell.

					Asset
	PEP	**Portfolio**	**Stock**	**Bond**	**Allocation**
Year	**BOLI**	**BOLI**	**BOLI**	**BOLI**	**BOLI**

Historical Analysis
Yield Comparison, 1974-1994

Year	PEP BOLI	Portfolio BOLI	Stock BOLI	Bond BOLI	Asset Allocation BOLI
1974	3.99	6.78	-25.46	-5.31	-13.17
1975	11.82	6.83	42.76	12.39	25.81
1976	12.99	6.83	38.36	16.40	24.67
1977	3.68	6.77	6.85	-0.54	3.84
1978	4.01	6.78	12.76	-2.32	6.67
1979	10.06	6.89	28.70	-6.43	14.05
1980	8.69	7.26	33.90	-5.01	17.25
1981	7.40	7.86	2.24	-3.49	2.56
1982	10.16	8.45	22.46	40.31	24.98
1983	13.51	8.83	28.84	4.01	16.93
1984	6.56	9.27	-2.45	14.61	4.68
1985	19.30	9.52	26.16	27.84	22.53
1986	11.08	9.59	10.41	17.60	11.27
1987	5.14	9.74	-4.29	-2.52	-2.25
1988	10.09	9.83	17.59	8.45	12.15
1989	18.89	9.79	18.59	13.98	14.71
1990	5.56	9.49	-14.62	4.53	-4.84
1991	18.33	8.91	35.34	17.64	23.63
1992	4.75	8.27	13.26	7.14	9.02
1993	5.99	7.74	13.24	10.94	10.03
1994	4.00	7.22	2.32	-2.25	-2.25
Average	9.22	8.21	13.22	7.39	10.06
Best	19.30	9.83	42.76	40.31	25.81
Worst	3.68	6.77	-25.46	-6.43	-13.17
Standard Deviation	*5.03*	*1.20*	*17.71*	*12.07*	*10.87*
Coefficient of Variation	0.55	0.15	1.34	1.63	1.08

Portfolio Life Insurance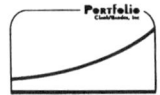

Portfolio life insurance products promise fixed-dollar benefits. The best types of assets to match this liability are fixed income securities. Since fixed-dollar benefit liabilities are backed by the general account, the insurance company invests a major portion of its general account assets in investment-grade bonds and mortgages.

For example, one life insurance company maintains a portfolio in its general account distributed as shown below:

Government Bonds 18.2%

Other Bonds 47.2%

Mortgages 20.0%

Stocks and Real Estate 1.2%

Cash and Cash Equivalents 1.1%

Policy Loans 12.3%

The bond quality of the company is weighted heavily toward the investment-grade end of the quality spectrum as illustrated by the following table:

AAA 36.8%

AA 12.2%

A 30.8%

BBB 17.8%

BB or lower 2.4%

This type of general account asset mix is fairly typical of financially strong life insurance companies.

Variable Life Insurance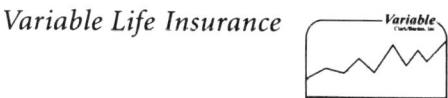

An insurance company typically maintains one separate account to hold the assets that support the liabilities generated by its variable life insurance policies. This is in addition to any other separate accounts it may maintain to support other variable-dollar benefit liabilities.

An owner of a variable life insurance policy can select investment subaccounts into which net premiums are to be deposited. The death benefit and cash value of a variable life insurance policy reflect the fair market value of the underlying investment subaccounts chosen by the policy owner.

A policy owner of a variable life insurance contract can choose any combination of investment subaccounts offered by the contract. In turn, an insurance company invests the assets of each subaccount in a corresponding investment fund. The investment funds are series type mutual funds registered with the Securities and Exchange Commission as open-end diversified management investment companies under the Investment Company Act of 1940. The policy owner, rather than the insurance company, determines the portfolio mix. Managers of the series funds control trading of securities, operating within the constraints of the investment objectives and policies set for the particular funds that they manage.

Protected Equity Plan® *(PEP)*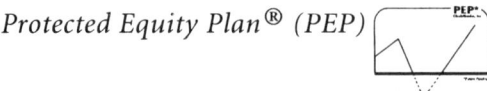

The Protected Equity Plan® (PEP) provides a return to the buyer equal to a specified percentage of the increase in the *Standard & Poor's 500 Stock Index,* subject to a floor minimum and a cap. PEP, like variable life plans, offers returns that are tied to the performance of a class of assets. Nevertheless, because of the floor guarantee, it is supported by an insurance company's general account, not by a separate account.

An insurance company can match these variable-like benefit liabilities in a number of ways. One approach is to set up a large equity portfolio within the general account to simulate the *Index.* However, that is not always possible because the company may not have enough investable assets to produce a basket of equities that would simulate the broad stock market. Such an inability to match could adversely affect the overall composition and quality rating of the insurance company's general account. Instead, the most efficient way to support the fluctuating obligations of PEP is to buy call options on the *Index.*

To support the minimum return guarantee, an insurance company places a large portion of its premium dollar — roughly 96 cents on the dollar in the interest rate environment prevailing at the time — in its general account. The interest earned on this portion of the premium is sufficient to meet the floor return guarantee. The remainder of the premium goes to pay for the following:

- Premium tax
- Deferred Acquisition Cost (DAC) tax
- Issue expenses
- Other expenses
- Call options on *Standard & Poor's 500 Stock Price Index*

The four cents per dollar of premium not invested in the general account will not cover all the expenses above. Thus, in addition to amortizing a portion of the taxes and expenses to be recovered in future years, an insurance company will also sell calls on the *Index* at a higher strike price than those it purchases. The net result is a spread which effectively supports a return cap.

It should be repeated that the promised return is tied to an outside index rather than an insurance company's own performance. Therefore, regardless of an insurance company's investment results, it must credit promised returns to PEP policies. If an insurance company does not hedge its exposure to PEP obligations, it is risking an asset and liability mismatch, something prudent insurance companies strive to avoid.

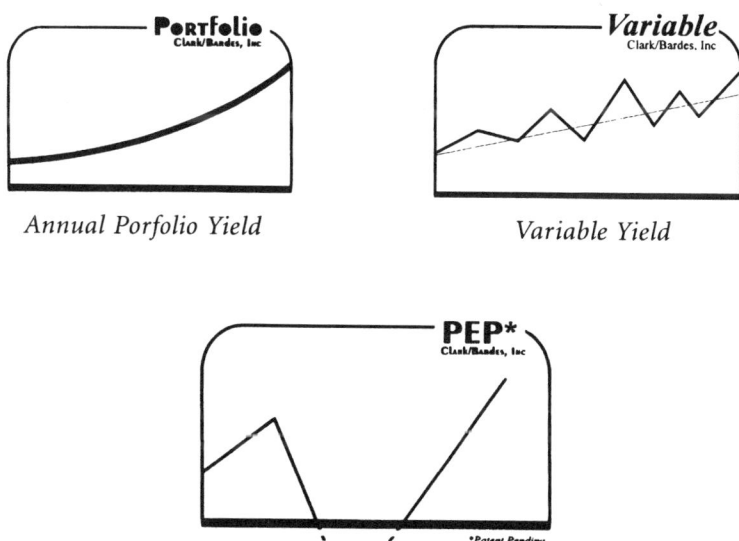

Annual Porfolio Yield

Variable Yield

Protected Equity Plan (PEP) *

The PEP policy has Patent Pending protection.

PRODUCT PRICING

The ultimate goal of product pricing is to ensure that the present value of future premiums is at least equal to the sum of the present values of benefit costs, policy expenses, allocated fixed expenses, and required profits.

When an insurance company develops a new product, the company's actuaries run the proposed product through a pricing model. Every insurance company has instituted its own profitability targets as measured by:

- Return on investment
- Premium margin
- Break-even year
- First year surplus strain

To the extent that the initial product design does not meet profitability objectives, actuaries and marketing specialists work jointly to modify the product design to optimize the trade-off between product appeal and profitability. The variables subject to change during this process are pricing assumptions and schedules for death benefits and cash values.

The expected timing of profits and losses must also be considered. The key variables to be considered on a block of new business include:

- Age and sex distribution
- Face amount distribution
- Risk distribution
- Policy lapses
- Mortality
- Investment returns
- Variable expenses
- Fixed expenses

Other factors that affect product pricing include an insurance company's reserving philosophy, sales goals, surplus position, and access to capital.

Deterministic and Stochastic Techniques of Pricing

Insurance companies use a variety of techniques in pricing products. These techniques can be categorized as either deterministic or stochastic. Many techniques combine elements of both methods.

A deterministic approach focuses on the most likely combination of future events based on past experience. The actuary bases his or her assumptions about what outcomes are likely in the future on an insurance company's experience with similar groups.

By contrast, a stochastic approach is based entirely on probability. An actuary makes assumptions about the statistical distribution underlying each variable. A random event generator is then developed to create a large number of possible scenarios based on assumed underlying distributions. Product profitability is calculated for each scenario. After perhaps 10,000 runs have been simulated, results can be plotted from which the actuary can develop fairly accurate projections of the profitability of the product. For example, the actuary may conclude there is a 90% probability that the ultimate profit for a proposed product will not be less than x million dollars and the first year loss will not exceed y million.

Of those techniques that combine the two approaches, the most common is a method in which an insurance company determines a set number of scenarios it considers to be most likely, assigning a probability to each. Profitability for each scenario is calculated. Based on the assigned probabilities, the insurance company calculates a probability-weighted profitability for the product. If the weighted profitability calculation meets all of the insurance company's targets, the product will be introduced.

PRODUCT CAPACITY

In the traditional marketplace, insurance companies try to maximize product sales. However, this is not the case in the BOLI market for two reasons: surplus strain and disintermediation risk.

Insurance companies typically suffer a first-year loss from the issuance of a new policy. The loss is the result of many one-time expenses associated with the sale of a policy, such as selling, underwriting, issuance, and record setup. An insurance company must have enough unallocated surplus to absorb these first-year losses. If not, it must limit its sales or accept a deterioration in its surplus position.

Under normal circumstances, no single buyer can purchase enough coverage to exhaust an insurance company's surplus set aside for new sales in a given year. However, in the BOLI market, an insurance company can easily exhaust an entire year's allocation of surplus in a few large transactions, preventing it from accepting any new business. Thus, an insurance company must divide its available surplus between its regular business and BOLI, effectively limiting the number of BOLI transactions in any one year.

Equally important in determining how much BOLI an insurance company may sell is potential disintermediation risk. Such risk is not an issue with variable life insurance because the value of the liability is equal to the value of the assets. Therefore, an insurance company is not at risk should it be forced to liquidate the assets to pay off its liabilities.

However, portfolio life insurance, which promises fixed-dollar benefits, does present disintermediation risk. Since an insurance company invests primarily in fixed-income securities, it faces disintermediation risk in a rising interest rate environment. Although asset values fluctuate, liabilities associated with portfolio insurance are measured at book value which never decrease, regardless of interest rates.

Thus, if a bank were to decide to cash in its BOLI program to take advantage of rising market interest rates, the insurance company would have to liquidate fixed-income securities in a rising interest rate environment, likely generating a capital loss. The gap between the book value of liabilities and the market value of assets would have to be made up from the insurance company's surplus, impairing the company's surplus position.

An insurance company can shorten the duration of its fixed income portfolio to reduce interest rate sensitivity. However, by going shorter on the yield curve, returns to BOLI buyers are reduced, diminishing the product's appeal.

Therefore, insurance companies in the BOLI market have placed limits on the amount of new business they will accept in any given year. The limits range from $100 million to $500 million of premium annually, depending on the surplus positions of the companies.

PRODUCT SELECTION

Product selection is a two-step process. First, a bank decides between portfolio, variable, or PEP programs. This is similar to an asset allocation decision. Second, the bank selects an insurance company or companies from which to buy. This is analogous to choosing specific securities for a portfolio.

Product chassis is not considered here because it does not determine product value. One product chassis does not inherently offer more value than another, but is simply a matter of the mechanics through which an insurance company structures insurance policies.

By making a decision to buy portfolio, variable, or PEP programs, a bank is expressing a preference for one of the following:

- Returns based on investment-grade fixed income securities measured at book value (portfolio)
- Returns from various investment securities to be selected by the financial institution measured at market value (variable)
- Combination return (PEP)

As noted before, expected yields of variable products rank first, if invested in riskier securities. The Protected Equity Plan® ranks second, followed by portfolio products. Higher expected yields come at the cost of more volatile returns. A bank could potentially find a place in its investment portfolio for any one or a combination of the three product classes, depending on its portfolio strategy and its existing asset mix.

CHAPTER 4
FINANCIAL PERFORMANCE
OF BOLI

This chapter discusses the historical and prospective yields of BOLI compared with traditional bank investments. BOLI is evaluated on both an after-tax and pre-tax basis. Since BOLI yields are income tax-free if policies are held to maturity, investment returns should be measured on a tax-free basis.

It is easy to construct the historical performance of BOLI. Life insurance carriers maintain careful performance records. For many life insurance carriers, their historical yield is a strong selling point. Carrier yields can be matched against yields from traditional bank investments to arrive at comparisons.

The chart on the following page compares, over a multiple year period, a type of traditional portfolio life insurance available through BOLI and a selection of traditional bank investments. BOLI has a yield advantage in every year.

BOLI's yield advantage is easy to understand. The insurance carrier is investing in seven to 10 year duration investments. The carrier passes on that yield —minus their charges —income tax-free.

While the data shows that BOLI offers higher yields than traditional bank investments, other considerations must be taken into account before setting up a BOLI plan. BOLI is different in some important respects from traditional bank investments in areas such as duration, liquidity and taxation.

ANNUAL PORTFOLIO YIELD BOLI VS
AFTER-TAX INVESTMENT YIELDS

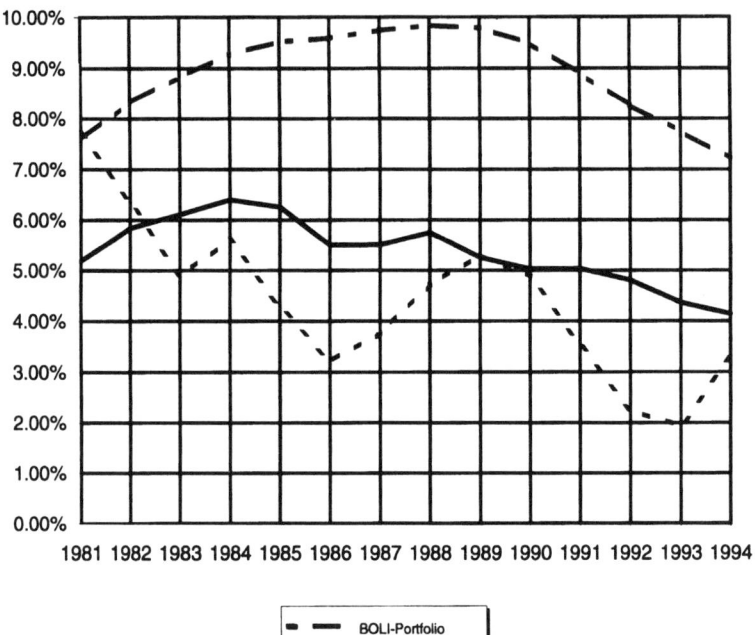

Assumption: BOLI was purchased in 1981.

DURATION

BOLI is a long term investment strategy. It is used to finance benefit costs which by their nature are long-term. In fact, benefit plan costs can effectively be considered permanent costs. As long as a bank is in business, it will have significant benefit costs. Therefore, the long term nature of BOLI is appropriate. In effect, BOLI can be viewed as a perpetual municipal with a yield that resets to the market annually. And, as yield comparisons demonstrate, the after-tax performance advantage of BOLI is favorable both in the short and long term.

LIQUIDITY

BOLI is a liquid investment. However, the best investment strategy is to hold BOLI to maturity when death proceeds are paid income tax-free. That makes the tax benefits permanent. Should coverage be terminated before the death of the insured, the cash value paid at surrender in excess of the premium is taxable as ordinary income to the bank. Therefore, it is to a bank's advantage to hold contracts to maturity. All the same, a tax-deferred yield is normally preferable to a yield that is taxable annually, just like tax-deferred annuities have advantages over certificates of deposit on any typical investment that is taxed annually.

Since the investment yield of BOLI is attractive in comparison to alternative bank investment opportunities, the liquidity issue should not normally arise. Banks would not ordinarily need to tap BOLI's cash value. Banks generally will not put more than 3% of their assets in BOLI. Therefore, BOLI should be considered a last-resort store of liquidity. Any bank that would have to turn to BOLI for liquidity would probably be experiencing earnings problems and not owe income taxes. Although surrender of BOLI would create a taxable event, that event would be immaterial since the bank would probably not be in a taxpaying status.

The issue of liquidity varies depending on the type of insurance policy the bank buys. Under the Internal Revenue Code, there are two methods of taxation applicable to life insurance contracts: the Non-Modified Endowment Contract and the Modified Endowment Contract. Appendix F has a complete legal description of each.

TAXATION: NON-MODIFIED ENDOWMENT CONTRACT

Under a Non-Modified Endowment Contract, a bank must pay at least four level annual premiums. The face amount of the insurance will be approximately 25 times the annual premium.

Under the contract, a bank can borrow on a nontaxable basis according to the policy's cash value. For example, if the cash value were $10 million, a bank would be able to borrow that amount from the carrier. The interest rate charged on loans is set annually and tied to the Moody's bond rate for seasoned corporate bonds.

Such loans are non-recourse and have no scheduled payback date. Loans can remain outstanding indefinitely, repaid when insured people die or when a policy is surrendered. Loans are not recorded as liabilities, but are netted against cash surrender values of contracts, which are bank assets. Therefore loans do not affect bank debt/equity ratios.

Loans are made by carriers against cash surrender values of the contracts and are nontaxable to the bank. Any interest earnings on premiums paid are also tax free. If a bank were to pay $10 million in premiums over four years and the cash value of a contract at the end of the fourth year were $13 million, the entire amount, including principal and interest, could be borrowed on an income tax-free basis.

Policy loan interest paid to a carrier is income-tax deductible up to $50,000 in loans per insured. Since banks pay no income tax on interest income paid on the policy, banks gain favorable advantage between interest income and interest expense. (Note: The Budget Reconciliation Act of 1995 would eliminate the deduction on policy loan interest by 1998.)

TAXATION:
MODIFIED ENDOWMENT CONTRACT

Under a Modified Endowment contract, a bank can pay as little as one premium. With a single premium contract, a bank will have a smaller death benefit in comparison to its premium. The average face amount may be only four to five times the premium. This reduced face amount helps a bank since it would pay a smaller mortality charge. Since a Modified Endowment Contract can still qualify as life insurance under the code and have a face amount which is less than that required with a Non-Modified Endowment Contract, the early year performance of the contract is superior, providing a higher first year cash value and, thus, yield.

However, the taxation of a Modified Endowment Contract is different. Loans taken against policy cash value are treated as interest income and are taxable. A 10% tax applies on loan interest earnings and upon surrender.

A reasonable question to ask is, should a bank simply buy Non-Modified Endowment Contracts in order to have access to policy cash value in a tax favored manner? The Non-Modified Endowment Contract has a higher face amount requirement and the corresponding mortality charges for additional death benefit. Moreover, the internal rate of return in the earlier years is lower.

For banks concerned about early yield, the Modified Endowment Contract clearly offers superior performance in the early years. If a bank does not expect to use BOLI contracts for liquidity, it is more advantageous to use a Modified Endowment Contract.

CHAPTER 5

HOW TO SELECT
A BOLI CARRIER

Once a bank has decided to set up a BOLI plan, it is vital to find a competitive and creditworthy insurance carrier or carriers. BOLI policies are not off-the-shelf products. Custom-tailored plan design and pricing are needed to achieve optimum results.

To serve the BOLI market, an insurance company must have a significant surplus. Among those carriers in a position to sell BOLI, only a few have made a commitment to the market or set up special departments to sell life insurance to banks. The relatively small number of providers makes selection simpler.

In choosing an insurance company, there are several factors that should be considered:

- Financial strength
- Plan type
- Pricing and projected returns
- Limits on policy amounts
- Account management
- Ability to administer BOLI

FINANCIAL STRENGTH

The most effective way to measure an insurance carrier is through rating systems designed by industry watchdogs, such as A.M. Best Company, Standard & Poor's, Moody's, and Duff & Phelps. Each firm has its own method of rating insurance companies. The following chart shows the rating systems used by each of the four:

INSURANCE CARRIER RATING AGENCIES AND RANKINGS

Ranking Level	A.M. Best*	Standard & Poor's**	Moody's***	Duff & Phelps*
1	A++	AAA	Aaa	AAA
2	A+	AA+	Aa1	AA+
3	A	AA	Aa2	AA
4	A-	AA-	Aa3	AA-
5	B++	A+	A1	A+
6	B+	A	A2	A
7	B	A-	A3	A-
8	B-	BBB+	Baa1	BBB+
9	C++	BBB	Baa2	BBB
10	C+	BBB-	Baa3	BBB-
11	C	BB+	Ba1	BB+
12	C-	BB	Ba2	BB
13	D	BB-	Ba3	BB-
14	E	B+	B1	B+
15	F	B	B2	B
16		B-	B3	B-
17		CCC	Caa	CCC
18		R	Ca	DD
19			C	

*Rating based on "Insurance Claims Paying Ability."

** Rating based on "Company's Financial Strength and Ability to Meet Obligations to Policyholders."

*** Rating based on "Degree of Investment Risk...Protected by a Stable Margin and Secure Principal."

Carriers rated in the top four levels have mini-
mal credit risk and are the best candidates to
select when making a BOLI purchase.

PLAN TYPE

Depending on its objectives, a bank can choose either a
fixed-yield or variable-yield plan. Some carriers specialize in
one type, some offer both, and some offer hybrid proprietary
plans such as the Protected Equity Plan®.

Insurance companies may design BOLI products in-house
or use consultants with specialized expertise. Products that
are backed by a carrier's general portfolio are usually designed
by the company's own actuaries. Variable products may be
designed in-house or by outside consultants. Hybrid forms
of BOLI are unusual and are normally designed by outside
firms.

It may be in the bank's interest to hire a broker
or consultant to assist in the design of hybrid
plans. A good BOLI consultant employs actuaries and other professionals who have the
specialized knowledge and skill which hybrid
products require. Consultants with proprietary
products have particular leverage in dealing with
insurance carriers.

PRICING

Pricing is a critical part of the design of a life insurance product. Setting prices is done in conjunction with the investment design portion of the plan. Figured into the price of a life insurance policy are mortality costs, cost of insurance, DAC taxes, fees, and commissions.

Carriers with large BOLI pools have the experience to price their products accurately. A newcomer to the market may be able to use its experience with other types of corporate life insurance to set prices.

When a carrier prices accurately, a bank's costs and benefits are optimized. If an insurance company underprices its product, a bank will not necessarily gain. The carrier may have to make up for the deficit in future years by increasing the cost of insurance. Funds used to make up for these shortcomings will reduce the amount of capital available for investment.

AMOUNT OF INSURANCE

Banks may only purchase insurance on the lives of their employees to offset the cost of employee benefits. The cost of the benefits is calculated on a present value basis over the working lifetimes of employees. This calculation is critical and, in performing it, advice from a consultant may be useful. A consultant can help ensure that a carrier is not inflating benefit costs to justify a higher premium.

A single carrier may not be able to supply a bank with the required amount of insurance. It is important to know a carrier's capacity before beginning purchase negotiations. Often, carriers have pledged a quantity of product exclusively to certain brokers. Working with such a broker can ensure access to a sufficient amount of insurance. A bank should consider signing an intent-to-purchase agreement as early as possible in negotiations. In case of limited supply, such an agreement will establish a bank's claim.

Most carriers write BOLI on a first come, first served basis. An aggressive insurance company courting top banks as BOLI clients may make exceptions. For example, it might steer a buyer into using a variable product, bypassing limits on use of the general account's surplus.

ACCOUNT MANAGEMENT

One of the most important factors in determining which carrier to select when purchasing BOLI is how accounts are managed. If a bank chooses a fixed-yield BOLI product, the investment is straightforward. The premium goes into a carrier's general account. Yield varies with the return on the insurance company's general investments. The carrier makes all the financial decisions for these investments.

If a bank purchases a variable-yield product in which it makes fund choices, it should check on investment fund management. Does the carrier manage investment funds in-house or does it use outside fund managers? There is considerable variation in the level of involvement of carriers in investment management. A bank can recommend an outside investment manager to the carrier. However, the bank may not exercise control over the investment manager's decisions.

If a bank is dissatisfied with investment results, it may have the option of surrendering its policies. But the disadvantages of surrender — especially the loss of tax benefits — makes such a move undesirable. Conflict can be avoided by discussing investment management with a carrier before a purchase is made.

PLAN ADMINISTRATION

The administrative duties of a carrier include processing death claims and program accounting. The latter is especially important because a bank needs accurate information about its account balance in order to report its earnings. Choosing a carrier with the ability to properly administer a plan is essential.

A consultant may sometimes be better equipped to administer an account than a carrier. A bank should look for an insurance company willing to work with a consultant in the ongoing administration of a BOLI plan.

CHAPTER 6

BOLI ACCOUNTING

Accounting is the process of identifying, measuring, recording, and communicating economic information to permit informed decisions by users of that information. When a bank makes a decision to purchase life insurance, it must comply with various regulatory accounting requirements. While most corporations are governed by Generally Accepted Accounting Principles (GAAP), banks are subject to additional accounting rules promulgated by state and federal bank regulatory agencies.

GENERALLY ACCEPTED ACCOUNTING PRINCIPLES (GAAP)

The American Institute of Certified Public Accountants (AICPA), the Financial Accounting Standards Board (FASB), and the Securities and Exchange Commission (SEC) are the agencies primarily responsible for developing GAAP. These accounting standards were developed to reduce inconsistencies in accounting practice and to improve the comparability and credibility of financial reports. Banks, like any other corporation, are required to prepare their financial statements in conformity with GAAP.

SECURITIES AND EXCHANGE COMMISSION

The SEC is an independent regulatory agency of the U.S. government which administers the Securities Act of 1933, the Securities Exchange Act of 1934, and other legislation. It is empowered to require corporate reports including the following:

- Registration statements required when companies make public offerings of securities

- 10-K Reports, filed annually, which include audited financial statements

- 10-Q Reports, filed quarterly, which include financial information for the period

- 8-K Reports, which explain events about which investors should be aware

The SEC requires all registrants to conform with GAAP. Regulation S-X contains the SEC's principle accounting guidelines. Article 4, Reg. 210.4-01(a)(1) states that:

> Financial statements filed with the Commission which are not prepared in accordance with generally accepted accounting principles will be presumed to be misleading or inaccurate...

According to GAAP, in reporting purchases of life insurance, changes in cash surrender value must be classified as adjustments to premium expense.

BANK REGULATORY AGENCIES

Banks are regulated by several state and federal agencies including the Office of the Comptroller of the Currency (OCC), the Federal Reserve System (Fed), the Federal Deposit Insurance Corporation(FDIC), and state banking departments. The Office of Thrift Supervision (OTS) has jurisdiction over savings institutions. These agencies issue charters and supervise commercial banks and thrifts.

Bank regulators have developed their own accounting regulations, referred to as Regulatory Accounting Principles (RAP), which can differ from GAAP. Bank regulators are concerned with safeguarding the safety and soundness of financial institutions and require certain financial information beyond that required by GAAP.

In some instances, RAP accounting methods are contrary to GAAP. In other instances, GAAP allows flexibility in accounting treatment, but RAP requires a specific method. Accounting for BOLI uses GAAP methods. There are no RAP guidelines that require treatment of BOLI different from that provided for by GAAP. However, state and federal bank regulatory agencies do stress the need to monitor an insurance carrier's financial condition on an ongoing basis.

ACCOUNTING FOR BOLI

Accounting for bank purchase of life insurance is relatively simple.[1] A bank identifies certain key executives or employees on whom it wishes to purchase life insurance. The bank is both the owner and beneficiary of the insurance policies. An insurance carrier is selected to provide the coverage in an amount determined to be in line with the risk of loss or the present value of future employee benefit costs. The bank can pay a single premium or annual premiums.

---

[1] Although not addressed in this chapter, risk-based capital guidelines are discussed in Appendix C. A Consolidated Income Statement before and after a BOLI purchase, including earnings-per-share increases, can be found in Appendix D.

Periodically the insurance carrier reports to the bank the cash surrender value of the policies. The cash surrender value represents the gross cash value of the policy, adjusted for expenses, accumulated dividends, interest, and prepaid premiums. The increase in cash surrender values is considered income for financial accounting purposes, but may be netted against premium expenses.

In the event of the death of an insured, the insurance carrier pays the bank the death proceeds. This is recorded as income. Because the death causes a corresponding decrease in the cash surrender value, the bank must reverse out the cash surrender value related to the policy that has matured.

OCC *BANKING CIRCULAR 249*
(See Appendix A)

The OCC has sought to ensure that banks purchase insurance products to fund employee benefits, not for investment purposes. In addition, the agency wants to limit unsecured cash surrender value as a percentage of a bank's capital. To address these issues, the OCC in 1991 issued *Circular 249* covering bank purchases of life insurance. This circular and FASB Technical Bulletin 85-4 are the guidelines banks use in making decisions about BOLI legal and accounting issues.

> *Circular 249* authorizes the use of life insurance as long as it is purchased in connection with employee compensation and benefit plans, as key-person insurance, life insurance on borrowers, or life insurance taken as security for loans. It does not authorize banks to purchase life insurance for their own accounts as investments.

While the main purpose of *Circular 249* was to address the legal guidelines under which a bank may purchase life insurance, the document also defines how the purchase of life insurance should be treated for accounting purposes. It states that life insurance death benefits and cash surrender values are unsecured obligations and should be reported as "Other Assets" on a bank's financial statement. This reflects the incidental nature of the asset. For most banks, the amount used to purchase life insurance is relatively small in relation to total bank assets. Recording it in the Other Assets category is therefore appropriate.

FASB TECHNICAL BULLETIN NO. 85-4
(See Appendix B)

FASB Technical Bulletin No. 85-4, titled *Accounting for Purchases of Life Insurance,* is the primary accounting guide. It is effective for insurance policies acquired after November 14, 1985. This bulletin evolved from a 1970 AICPA accounting interpretation entitled *Accounting for Key-Man Life Insurance* which identified the cash surrender value method as generally accepted accounting for purchases of life insurance. In 1984, as new types of life insurance were introduced, the bulletin was reviewed. The AICPA's Accounting Standards Executive Committee reaffirmed support of the cash surrender value method in the October 1984 issues paper entitled, "Accounting for Key-Person Life Insurance."

Under the Cash Surrender Value (CSV) method, premium payments are expensed and cash surrender value increases are reported as income.

Premium payment could be a one-time annual expense or may be amortized monthly over a period of one year. For example, if a premium were paid at the first of the year, a bank would credit cash and debit insurance expense. It also could credit cash and debit a prepaid insurance expense account and amortize the insurance expense monthly over the entire year.

A bank regularly receives a statement from its insurance carrier stating BOLI cash surrender value. This may be reported as a credit to other income and a debit to the CSV asset account. In practice, the policy premium is often netted against the cash value increase to create net life insurance expense or income.

When an insured employee dies, the death proceeds from the policy are recorded as income and the accruals of cash value are reversed. Some banks use different account names in which they record income from increases in policy cash surrender values. These can include BOLI income, employee benefit income, tax exempt income, or other income.

In the following example, Bank X purchases a $200,000 single premium life insurance policy on an employee's life. At the end of year ten, the employee dies. The bank would make the following accounting entries.

SAMPLE INSURANCE ACCOUNTING ENTRIES

SINGLE EMPLOYEE RISK ASSUMED
AT END OF YEAR TEN

Accounting Year	Insurance Expense (Premium)	Annual Cash Surrender Value Increase	Death Benefit	Net Life Insurance Income (Expense)	Balance Sheet Total (Cash Surrender Value)
1	($51,478)	$54,310	0	$2,832	$54,310
2	0	$2,824	0	$2,824	$57,134
3	0	$2,684	0	$2,684	$59,818
4	0	$2,808	0	$2,808	$62,626
5	0	$3,254	0	$3,254	$65,880
6	0	$3,322	0	$3,322	$69,202
7	0	$3,496	0	$3,496	$72,698
8	0	$3,674	0	$3,674	$76,372
9	0	$3,866	0	$3,866	$80,238
10	0	$4,054	0	$4,054	$84,292
Death		($84,292)	$200,000	$115,708	
	($51,478)	$0	$200,000	$148,522	$0

TAXATION OF BANK OWNED LIFE INSURANCE

Ignoring alternative minimum tax considerations, cash surrender value accumulations and death proceeds are not subject to income tax if policies are held until the deaths of insured persons. Conversely, premium payments are not deductible. In FASB 109, *Accounting for Income Taxes,* paragraph 14 specifies that the excess of cash surrender value of life insurance over premiums paid is a temporary difference if the cash surrender value is expected to be recovered by surrendering the policy. It is not a temporary difference if the asset is expected to be recovered without tax consequence upon the death of the insured.

Banks generally intend to hold insurance policies until the deaths of the insured, leaving policy income free of tax. If a bank were to change its intention, deferred taxes would be recorded for the temporary difference.

ALTERNATIVE MINIMUM TAX CONSIDERATIONS

Under regular tax rules, life insurance proceeds are excluded from gross income and therefore are income tax free to the beneficiary. Likewise, the inside buildup of life insurance cash value is excluded from gross income so long as it is left in the policy. A bank should calculate its taxes twice each year, once under the regular tax rules and once under the Alternative Minimum Tax (AMT) rules. The bank then would pay taxes based on whichever calculation produces the higher tax amount.

To calculate its alternative minimum tax, a bank first calculates its alternative minimum taxable income (AMTI) which is regular taxable income with some adjustments and increases due to tax preference items such as accelerated depreciation. It also calculates its adjusted current earnings (ACE). The ACE adjustment is intended to reflect the corporation's pre-tax net book income as measured for financial accounting purposes. Its purpose is to ensure that a corporation which reports a profit to the public or its shareholders reports that profit to the IRS as well. A bank or corporation must increase its AMTI by 75% of the amount by which ACE exceeds AMTI (or reduce its AMTI by 75% of the amount by which ACE falls short of AMTI).

Regulations set guidelines on the effect of BOLI on adjusted current earnings (ACE). The income included in ACE differs depending on activity related to the insurance contract during the year. If a bank maintains the insurance contract and pays an annual premium, the income for ACE purposes for the year is calculated by taking the cash surrender value at the end of the year, minus the sum of the cash surrender value at the end of the prior year plus the premiums paid during the year. This amount is reported as part of adjusted current earnings.

For example, if the cash surrender value at the end of year one were $12,000, at the end of year two $15,000, and the premium paid $2,500, the ACE income for year two would be $500 ($15,000-[$12,000+$2,500]). Calculations would change if there were death proceeds or distributions during the year.

While cash value buildup and death proceeds affect the ACE adjustment, they do not necessarily subject the bank to AMT. Life insurance is only one of many factors that determine whether a bank must pay an AMT. However, it is possible that life insurance death benefits and cash value increases, when added to other AMT preference items, could be enough to make a bank subject to AMT.

Any AMT tax paid may be carried forward for an unlimited period as a credit against taxes payable in future years under the regular tax calculation. Thus, AMT is not an additional tax but, rather, a temporary tax that creates only a timing difference.

FINANCIAL STATEMENT DISCLOSURE

There is nothing in SEC Regulation S-X or GAAP that requires disclosure related to bank owned life insurance. A bank may choose to disclose information about its Other Asset account at its discretion. Several recent annual reports from banks that had purchased life insurance included no disclosure about BOLI programs. Life insurance transactions are considered immaterial and do not require supportive information.

As banks increase purchases of insurance products, accounting issues will draw more attention. There may be increased demand for disclosure. The purchase of life insurance by a bank is a unique transaction and differs significantly from purchase of other kinds of assets.

Financial executives at banks that have purchased life insurance note that, in the beginning, accountants and bank auditors have to be walked through transactions in order to understand the activity. For most banks, ownership of life insurance is a new phenomenon. Many have not booked a death proceed.

In fact, life insurance provides significant benefits to a bank and involves simple accounting procedures. The value of BOLI's tax-favored treatment of cash buildup and death benefits coupled with its utility as a funding source for employee benefit programs makes the product very attractive. It promises a positive impact on the balance sheet, the income statement, and, most importantly, shareholders.

CHAPTER 7

LEGAL ASPECTS OF BOLI

The decision by a bank to purchase life insurance must be based on strategy, economics, taxes, and the legal impact of BOLI. Three key legal questions are:

- What constitutes an insurable interest?
- What are the requirements of OCC *Banking Circular 249?*
- How do BOLI and tax deductions for interest on bank indebtedness affect the bank?

INSURABLE INTEREST

The question of a bank's insurable interest in the lives of its employees is one of the most significant legal issues surrounding BOLI. Current law holds that banks can have a legitimate interest in insuring employees' lives, making the purchase of bank owned life insurance a legal transaction.

Statutory and case law define precisely what constitutes an insurable interest. For more than a century, the U.S. Supreme Court has held that an insurable interest:

> ...may be stated generally...to be such an interest, arising from the relations of the party obtaining the insurance, either as creditor of or surety for the assured, or from the ties of blood or marriage to him, as will justify a reasonable expectation of advantage or benefit from the continuance of his life. It is not necessary that the expectation of advantage or benefit should be

> always capable of pecuniary estimation...
> *Warnock v. Davis, 104 U.S. 775, 779 (1881).*

This definition recognizes the court's discretion in determining which relationships create an insurable interest. That flexibility is limited by the interests of public policy which dictate against creating an interest in the early death of an insured. For a person or entity to acquire insurance on the life of another, the policyholder must reasonably expect to benefit from the continuance of the life of the insured. *Warnock, 104 U.S. at 779.*

These general requirements have created a broad class of relationships which have been held to support the existence of an insurable interest. The rules controlling the construction and application of insurable interests vary somewhat among individual states, but they are broadly similar and consistent with the Supreme Court's decision in Warnock.

Once the requirements for insurable interest are satisfied, the policy remains valid even if the beneficiary does not have an insurable interest at the time of the death of the insured. *44 C.J.S. Insurance Sec.175c.* The United States Supreme Court has traditionally held that an originally valid life insurance policy does not cease to be so with the cessation of the beneficiary's interest in the life of the insured, unless so provided in the policy itself. *Grigsby v. Russell, 222 U.S. 149 (1911).*

With few limitations, each person is considered to have an insurable interest in his or her own life and may designate any beneficiary, even though the beneficiary does not have an insurable interest in the life of the insured. *44 C.J.S. Insurance Sec.202; Couch on Insurance 2d Sec.24:115.* An insurable interest also exists in close family relationships, such as relationships between spouses, parents and children, siblings, and engaged couples. The law recognizes that individual autonomy

76

and ties of blood and marriage support personal insurable interests.

INSURABLE INTEREST IN
BUSINESS RELATIONSHIPS

The law also recognizes that certain business relationships give rise to insurable interests. Obviously, such a relationship exists between creditors and debtors, and most employers have an insurable interest in the lives of key employees whose services are critical to the success of the business and whose death would create a substantial loss to the business.

The law concerning an employer's ability to insure the life of a non-key employee performing ordinary services cannot be stated so succinctly. Generally, an employer does not have an insurable interest in the life of an employee based solely on the employment relationship when the employee is not considered a key employee. *Gerald v. Metropolitan Life, 168 Miss. 207 (1933)*. However, certain circumstances in common employment relationships may give rise to an insurable interest even for a non-key employee.

When an employer is able to demonstrate a responsibility, based on custom, to provide medical and death benefits to employees, the employer is considered to have an insurable interest. *Neely v. Pigford, 181 Miss. 306 (1938)*. Similarly, when the employer has a legal responsibility to provide its employees medical benefits, an insurable interest may also exist. *Bauer v. Bates Lumber Co., Inc., 503 P.2d 1169 (N.M.App. 1972), cert. den. 83 N.M. 390*.

These cases demonstrate the trend toward judicial recognition of an insurable interest of an employer in the life of an employee when the employer is exposed to liability for future medical, death, disability, or pension benefits. In fact, the law concerning insurable interests in such circumstances has been codified by statute in many states.

While differences exist between these statutes, the law generally holds that a business can have an insurable interest in the lives of its employees for the purpose of funding certain benefits, provided that proceeds of the insurance do not exceed the benefit obligation of the company. Consequently, bank owned life insurance represents a legally recognized means for banks to finance their growing benefit obligations.

OCC *BANKING CIRCULAR 249*
(See Appendix A)

Many conditions governing BOLI stem from the requirements of OCC *Banking Circular 249*. The circular provides general guidelines for national banks to determine whether they may legally purchase particular life insurance products. Among the circular's provisions is one allowing banks to purchase life insurance to finance employee benefit plan obligations. State-chartered banks supervised by the Federal Reserve or the FDIC must follow broadly similar rules.

This circular was published in 1991 in response to OCC's concern over the investment nature of the cash surrender value of life insurance and the potential risk of such unsecured assets to a banks' capital.

The circular stated the OCC's interpretation that federal banking statutes do not permit banks to purchase life insurance as an investment. However, banks may purchase life insurance if the purpose is incidental to the operation of their businesses. This occurs in two circumstances: insurance for key employees and insurance to finance employee compensation or benefits.

Test A

The first circumstance, called "Test A," under which the circular permits a bank to purchase life insurance is to protect itself against the loss of key employees. Generally, a bank may purchase life insurance on the life of any officer or director of the bank whose death would be sufficiently damaging to the bank to create an insurable interest in his or her life.

> The bank's board of directors is required to document the basis for determining which employees are key persons and the amount of insurance needed to indemnify the bank against the death of such persons. The bank may not purchase life insurance for an employee who cannot be demonstrated to be key to its business nor can the bank purchase an amount in excess of its potential loss.

The circular also states that the bank's authority to hold life insurance on key employees terminates if the employee ceases to be a key person due to retirement, discharge, or some other event. Therefore, the economic effect of terminating or transferring life insurance policies must be evaluated carefully on an individual basis under Test A.

This provision of the circular also allows a bank to purchase life insurance on the life of borrowers under certain circumstances, depending on applicable state law. Such policies must comply with the restrictions discussed above. They may not be used by a bank as a method to recover obligations that have been or are expected to be written off.

Test B

The second circumstance under which *Circular 249* permits banks to purchase life insurance, "Test B," is in connection with certain compensation agreements and benefit plan obligations.

Banks are given discretion in establishing compensation levels and benefit plans, though both must be justified. The circular provides that life insurance is a legally acceptable means for a bank to finance such obligations.

Benefit plans discussed in the circular include traditional employee benefits and director fee deferral programs, but not estate management programs for key employees except as part of reasonable compensation. Life insurance purchased in connection with compensation agreements and benefit plans may be held as long as a bank has a continuing liability under such plans. The OCC allows calculations under Test B to be performed on an aggregate or group basis. In other words, an individual policy need not be used to finance an individual employee's benefit.

A bank also may take an interest in life insurance policies as security for loans. The circular holds that life insurance death benefits and cash surrender values are unsecured assets of the bank. Cash surrender value of insurance should be reported in the Other Asset line on the bank's financial statement.

OCC *Banking Circular 249* is a concise statement of the requirements for BOLI contained in regulations, letters and interpretive rulings. Banks should carefully evaluate the economic and tax consequences of purchasing such insurance, but the thrust of the circular is to confirm that BOLI remains an approved legal option.

IRC SEC. 264
(See Appendix E. Also see IRC Sec. 7702, Life Insurance Contract Defined, Appendix F)

Another issue concerning BOLI is the effect of insurance on a bank's ability to take a tax deduction for interest paid on its indebtedness. Although the Internal Revenue Service has not issued a definitive statement on this issue, existing law holds that banks may continue to deduct interest paid on normal indebtedness, but not on indebtedness incurred specifically to purchase life insurance.

In general, no tax deduction is allowed for amounts paid as premiums for a life insurance policy nor for interest paid on indebtedness directly or indirectly related to the purchase of life insurance. *IRC Sec. 264(a).* This rule applies equally to BOLI and life insurance purchases by individuals or other businesses.

The IRC provisions are not specific as to what is necessary to establish a relationship between borrowing and the purchase of a life insurance policy. Certainly, where a debt is incurred for the specific purpose of purchasing life insurance, a direct relationship is established. The question of what constitutes an indirect relationship has been much debated. It can be argued that bank funds spent to purchase insurance represent the diminution of a scarce resource, cash, that indirectly creates the need for borrowing to finance other expenditures. But the weight of authority establishes that IRC Sec. 264 is not intended to do away with the deduction for interest where its relationship to life insurance is so remote.

The clearest evidence of the purpose of IRC Sec.264 is recorded in a discussion that took place in the U.S. Senate between Senator Smathers of Florida and Senator Long of Louisiana concerning a similar provision in the Revenue Act of 1964. (*1964 Congressional Record 2325,2326.*) This discussion demonstrates that the legislative intent of the Act was to eliminate only the interest deduction for borrowing clearly related to the purchase of life insurance.

The legislators' purpose was not to do away with the deductibility of interest payments for taxpayers who also happen to own life insurance. Senator Long clearly stated that the mere purchase of insurance is not in itself a basis for disallowing the deductibility of interest on normal indebtedness. Only interest that is related by some systematic scheme to the purchase of life insurance is disallowed, the senator noted.

The key issue in determining whether indebtedness is related to the purchase of life insurance is the intention of the borrower. If the borrowing can be easily traced to a specific purchase of life insurance, then interest is not deductible. If borrowing took place in the ordinary course of business, however, the deduction is likely to be allowed.

The fact that a bank makes an economic choice in order to utilize scarce resources to purchase life insurance does not determine the status of indebtedness incurred subsequent to the purchase even if it were made necessary because other resources were exhausted in the purchase of the life insurance. There must be an intentional relationship between the subsequent indebtedness and the original purchase based on a systematic plan.

Among the factors that indicate the intent of the borrower is the method of recording the debt in the bank's financial statements and accounting records. Internal correspondence and board of directors minutes can also demonstrate a bank's intent.

The mere existence of a life insurance policy among a bank's assets does not eliminate the deductibility of interest on indebtedness, unless the indebtedness is directly or indirectly related by an identifiable plan to the purchase of the insurance.

Though the legal issues associated with BOLI vary from state to state and under specific circumstances, such insurance generally represents an attractive option for financing benefit obligations. The law surrounding insurable interests, *Banking Circular 249,* and IRC Sec. 264 provide guidance for banks considering the purchase of life insurance. BOLI is consistent with legal requirements and does not raise unduly complex or difficult legal problems.

The Theory and Practice of Bank Owned Life Insurance

CHAPTER 8
ADMINISTRATION
OF BOLI PLANS

A consultant can advise on the design and purchase of an effective BOLI plan. Similarly, a consultant can perform the equally important function of administering the plan.

The administration of BOLI encompasses the enrollment process, the initial policy delivery and plan review, and on-going maintenance of the program. Many banks hire the same firms that helped design and purchase the plans to serve as program administrators.

A good administrator should have adequate computing systems and legal, actuarial and accounting expertise. The long term viability of the consulting organization must also be considered. Most BOLI transactions are front-end loaded, which means most of the consultant's revenue comes in the early years of the plan. A consulting company should have procedures in place to ensure that sufficient revenue is gained from administration. Otherwise, the firm's viability depends on new sales.

The ideal consultant not only displays ingenuity in design, but also commitment to its administrative staff and systems. Administration should be an independent profit center not dependent upon future sales. Before a consultant is chosen, bank personnel should visit the candidate's administrative unit to inspect its operations and interview the people who would be involved in administering the BOLI plan.

ENROLLMENT

The first administrative step in BOLI is enrollment. Using an experienced consultant is advisable, particularly when multiple sites are involved. Although bank personnel will be involved in the enrollment process, a consultant provides manpower and expertise, prevents errors, and saves time and money.

An administrative consultant should begin by setting up a pre-enrollment planning meeting. The bank's human resources director, compliance officer, financial officer, and any other personnel who will be involved in enrollment should attend.

The enrollment plan should address the following:

1. Consent of the insured

2. Enrollment timing

3. Corporate culture and perception of the plan

4. Enrollment communication

Consent

Depending on state requirements and the bank's needs, the issue of the consent of insured employees must be addressed. Three consent variations include:

- Full or positive consent: each insured must elect to be insured
- Notification: each proposed insured is notified that the bank wishes to insure his or her life and given reasonable time to decline
- No consent: the bank does not notify employees of its intent to insure their lives

Other enrollment steps will vary depending on the consent requirements of the state. For plan consent purposes, the location of the corporate headquarters office determines which state procedures must be followed.

Enrollment Timing

The bank determines the best policy date, taking into consideration fiscal year end, the timing of the premium payment, budget projection needs, and similar considerations. Once a date is set, the bank and the consultant construct an enrollment timeline. (See Appendix G for a typical BOLI implementation timetable.)

Corporate Culture

If an outside consultant is retained, the bank should inform the consultant about sensitivities in the employee population. For example, sometimes a simple word choice such as "officer," "employee," or "executive" can project an unintentional message. Heavy turnover, job cutbacks, reductions in benefits and similar factors should be considered as communications are developed in order to foster a positive perception of the plan.

Enrollment Communication

Giving prospective insured employees advance notice of the bank's request and an explanation of the bank's motivation can boost participation rates. In organizations that have implemented BOLI plans, over 95% of all eligible employees have voluntarily agreed to participate.

Communication about BOLI depends on which employees are included in the plan — all employees, or just officers and executives. An important concern is how best to communicate to employees about a plan that insures their lives, but does not provide them any death benefits. The answer is to emphasize that BOLI helps the employer offer competitive benefits.

Most BOLI plans are issued on a "Guaranteed Issue" basis, which means that all participants are included regardless of health as long as the human resources department certifies to the carrier that all insured participants are actively employed on the date of application and have not missed more than five consecutive days in the last 90 days due to illness.

The introductory communication to employees is usually a one-page letter from a bank officer explaining the plan and its benefits. (See sample communication letters in Appendix H.) To help encourage enrollment, it is important to use bank colors and logos on enrollment materials and consent cards that match those used with other bank-sponsored plans. The consultant should review the design of the material, which must be approved by the bank and the insurance carrier. (See Appendix I for sample Consent Cards).

Distribution and Collection System for Consent Cards

The appointment of site coordinators for each division or location improves accountability and, consequently, participation rates. In this method of distribution, each coordinator is mailed a package of enrollment materials and a census of eligible employees at his or her location. The coordinator is responsible for distributing the materials and collecting consent cards.

The bank gives the coordinator use of the interoffice mail system and schedules group or individual meetings. All locations should be instructed about any special methods to be used.

The site coordinators are responsible for auditing and reconciling the consent cards with the census. The coordinators then mail the cards back to a central location at the bank or consultant's office.

On receiving the cards, the consultant audits them for completeness and reconciles them with the original census of eligible employees. A report is prepared detailing the number of positive, negative, and no responses received. Based on this information, the bank decides whether follow-up enrollments are necessary.

Policy Issue

Once enrollment is complete, the consultant organizes the completed cards and forwards them to the insurance carrier for processing. Policies are then issued by the insurance carrier and sent to the consultant. The consultant audits the policies for accuracy. Once the audit is complete and the necessary adjustments made, the policies are placed in the administrator's electronic data systems. An "as sold" financial analysis is run to compare the actual program to the version originally proposed. When this analysis is completed, the consultant schedules a meeting with the bank to deliver the policies and review the plan.

INITIAL ADMINISTRATION MEETING

An initial administration meeting should be scheduled soon after receipt of the policy contracts. This meeting should cover all bank concerns and establish a working relationship between the consultant and the bank's in-house administrative contact. The outside administrator should be informed about the bank's reporting requirements for the plan.

The initial administration meeting usually covers the following topics:

Overview of the Plan

It is likely that some bank personnel who will be part of the internal administration of the plan were not involved in the bank's decision to purchase the BOLI plan. All involved parties should be briefed on the purpose and design of the plan, both short term and long term.

Policy Delivery

The policies are issued as one policy per life, or grouped together by age and sex and issued on an aggregate basis. The bank should verify the terms of the policy contract by requesting a specimen policy from the carrier. The specimen is reviewed at the meeting. The bank's legal counsel also reviews the terms.

The policies themselves should be stored separately from personnel records of insured employees in order not to be mistaken for employee benefits. The location of the policies should be noted in an administration manual for future reference.

Review of Sample Reports

The consultant explains the types of reports that can be provided to help the bank manage the plan. These reports include cash values, death benefits, inventoried policies (on terminated insureds), deceased insureds, and other relevant material. The bank chooses which reports it wants and specifies how they should be customized.

Reporting Calendar

An important function of the initial administration meeting is to establish a timetable for reporting plan performance.

Although there is a standard set of data that all BOLI purchasers need, the reports should be tailored based on such variables as organizational structure, the relationship of the policy date to the bank's fiscal year, the timing of the bank's budgeting cycle, and other bank requirements. It should be clearly established which bank staff member should receive each report.

Review of "As Sold" Illustration

An illustration detailing the financial impact of the plan is presented. This illustration projects the performance of the plan based on the specific lives insured, comparing the purchased plan with any previous illustrations presented during the marketing stage. Any variances must be explained.

Presentation of Administration Manual

The consultant provides the bank with an administration manual which:

- Documents the history and design of the BOLI plan, including policies issued, program design, population insured, assumptions used in the original financial analysis, and any other important information
- Specifies the reports needed by the bank and the reporting calendar
- Provides the administrator's name, address, and phone number
- Identifies a central location where the bank can store BOLI plan data
- Outlines procedures to be followed in cases of death of insured employees

At the conclusion of this meeting, the bank's internal BOLI administrators should be familiar with the status of the plan. They should have a list detailing the delivery schedule for reports, identifying the individuals at the bank who receive them. Bank staff members must know their contact person at the consultant's office for ongoing administrative issues and a backup person when the primary contact is unavailable.

MANAGEMENT REPORTS

Management reports for a BOLI program must be straightforward and easy to understand. As explained above, the bank agrees with the consultant on each report's due date and the identity of the bank staff member to whom each should be sent.

Reports include:

Census Reconciliation

If the human resources department is responsible for enrollment, it uses this report to track consent agreements. The report lists which eligible employees gave consent, monitoring each one until policies are issued.

List of Comprehensive Policy Information

This is an inventory of policies issued, including their initial premium and death benefit. The report is used as a benchmark.

Accounting Entries

These reports are provided to the appropriate accounting division on a schedule determined by the bank.

Premium Invoice

Most BOLI plan designs have a single invoice for the first policy year and no future billings. However, BOLI plans can have widely varying premium payment schedules. At a minimum, the invoice includes policy numbers, the names of insured employees, and premium amounts due.

Cash Surrender Values

The components of policy cash values are prepared for the bank on a scheduled basis. These reports provide information needed by the bank to properly book the insurance asset. The reports present information according to policy number. If the bank requires, the report provides subtotals by subsidiary.

Death Benefit Reports

The total death benefit amount for each policy, including its components, are prepared on a scheduled basis. Although death benefit amounts can change daily, the reports provide a rough idea of claim amounts when insured employees die.

Financial Projections

The projected financial impact of the plan on the bank should be prepared annually. This report projects performance of the plan for its remaining life. It illustrates changes in projected performance due to policy crediting rate changes or other changes.

Miscellaneous Reports

Other reports, such as insureds' beneficiary reports for the bank, reports on paid death benefits (if a death benefit is offered to the consenting insureds), and reports on deceased insureds or terminated insureds are prepared as needed.

PLAN TRANSACTION PROCESSING

The primary processing items in a BOLI plan are the initial premium invoice, death claims, and tracking of terminated insured employees.

Premium Invoice

Many BOLI plans have single premiums, although some carry multiple premiums. To preserve policy values as of a given date prior to final premium calculation, a bank may remit an estimated premium using a preliminary census. If consent of insureds is not needed, the estimate may coincide with the final premium. However, when consent is required, a premium reconciliation is necessary when policies are issued. If the plan calls for multiple premiums, the bank is notified in advance of premium due dates and wire transfer instructions are given.

Death Claims

The consultant acts as an intermediary to expedite the processing of death claims. A typical death claim process begins when a bank notifies its consultant that a death has occurred in the insured population. The bank forwards a certified death certificate to the consultant. The consultant then prepares the appropriate documents, attaches the death certificate and forwards the material to the insurance carrier. If the insurance carrier requires additional information, it notifies the consultant.

Terminated Insureds

Since BOLI policies are generally kept in force on terminated employees, a bank must keep track of the post-termination status of former employees. The consultant contracts with a company that conducts social security sweeps and collects death benefit records from federal and state agencies. The consultant should alternate between two or more services since most get information from different sources and may have slightly different data. The consultant informs the bank of deaths of former employees and prepares necessary documents for the insurance carrier.

ANALYSIS SERVICES

At least once a year, a bank and its consultant should meet to review the performance of a BOLI plan. This analysis includes examination of historical plan performance against client objectives, as well as recommendations for reevaluation of strategy. It should encompass policy performance in dividends and interest, actual versus expected death claims experience, and corporate tax assumptions. When data indicate a strategy change, the consultant makes recommendations to the bank.

The best way to carry out the analysis is to use a reprojection system which includes both insurance accounting and financial applications. A good reprojection system considers the entire BOLI product design, including the insurance carrier's rates, fees, interest and dividend history. These are measured against the parameters of each policy in the plan. This information is used to project financial values for each policy until maturity. The projections for each policy are combined to form a composite for the entire group.

Information on actual death claims, expected death claims, loans, withdrawals, and corporate tax rates is used to construct a variety of reports. These reports cover cash flow, profits and losses, and the performance of separate policy components. In addition, the internal rate of return of the entire BOLI plan is forecast. The bank must receive this information at least once a year to compare expected performance with actual results. The reprojection system should permit the bank to evaluate results on a quarterly or yearly basis.

VALIDATION OF VALUES AND RECORDKEEPING

The systems to validate and store carrier values are at the heart of proper plan administration. A consultant must be able to obtain current and projected values from the system so that a bank does not have to depend on the carrier for such information. Too often carriers make subtle mistakes in entering policies in their systems or in adding new data. Unless an independent source audits the values, mistakes can go undetected. In addition, the consultant should be able to generate customized reports that the carrier may not offer. These can include historical values, current values, and projected values. The items that should be tracked are:

- Policy cash values, broken into the appropriate components
- Policy death benefit, by components
- Premium paid
- Dividends paid
- Withdrawals and partial surrenders
- Death proceeds paid

Historical policy records are used in plan analysis to document trends in performance. Current values are used for accounting and management reports. Projected values are used for budget purposes and for analyzing expected performance.

TAX AND LEGAL CONSIDERATIONS

Periodically, tax and regulatory agencies revise their interpretations of the treatment of insurance and benefit plans. The bank must keep abreast of these changes in order to receive the most favorable tax treatment for its BOLI plan. A consultant normally tracks such changes, notifying the bank when appropriate.

DATA SYSTEMS

A BOLI plan represents a substantial investment for a bank. The plan uses confidential information, such as employee salary amounts. The values of the policies in the plan are also confidential and should be safeguarded. A consultant must store data on a secure system with appropriate backups and disaster-recovery procedures.

The software used to prepare reports should be customized so that a change in client strategy can easily be accommodated. Data systems fall into two categories: projection systems described above under "Analysis Services" and administrative systems. Administrative systems include information for each policy on premium payments, death benefit amounts, cash value amounts, death claims, loans, loan interest, withdrawals, and general information on the insured. This information can be transferred from the insurance carrier's system and modeled in ways not provided by the carrier. The consultant's system should be able to accommodate values from the insurance carrier at any point in the year, not just on an annual basis.

Although historical data generally should be kept separate from projected data, the reprojection system must be able to accept historical data on the BOLI plan for use in forecasting financial results. The reprojection system is used for financial reporting purposes separate from administrative requirements.

When possible, the bank should establish an electronic mail link with the consultant to facilitate communication. The consultant and bank can use their computer systems to exchange routine information.

CHAPTER 9

PARTNERING FOR SUCCESS: HOW TO CHOOSE A CONSULTANT

After reading this book, a bank official may believe that he or she is well prepared to successfully implement a BOLI plan. Nevertheless, the assumption that a bank can do so on its own may not be accurate. A critical part of a successful plan is the selection of a consultant who can guide a bank through each phase of the program. This selection marks the beginning of a partnership which will grow over the life of a plan.

THE NEED FOR A CONSULTANT

A BOLI plan is complex. There are many aspects that require expert attention. Optimal execution requires expertise in a number of different areas. A good consultant will provide the necessary expertise.

> Developing this knowledge base requires resources and time. Unless a bank is willing to develop its own expertise, the only viable alternative is to purchase these services. With a transaction of the size and importance of a BOLI plan, a reliable and highly regarded consulting firm is needed.

Another important reason for choosing a consultant is to obtain leverage in carrier relationships. Although carriers value client relationships, they do not work for a bank. Carriers are selling products. Their goal is to maximize profits while maintaining a competitive edge. Even the competitive advantage gained through product performance is less important to carriers than maintaining their industry ratings. Ratings are their lifeblood and an important competitive advantage. Insurance carriers have complete latitude in determining the competitiveness of their products. At any time, they can increase their spreads and lower a bank's yields.

Leverage with carriers also extends to obtaining the product itself. In an active market such as that for BOLI, demand often exceeds supply. For consultants, firmly established relationships in the industry allow them to negotiate and deliver the best possible products to buyers.

> A single purchaser possesses little leverage in negotiating with carriers. With limited product availability, there are more potential buyers than willing sellers. A bank needs an advocate working on its behalf who represents a large body of buyers and can negotiate more favorably with suppliers. An effective consultant functions on behalf of the bank much like a powerful and respected consumer advocate.

THE ROLE OF THE CONSULTANT

Understanding the role of the consultant is important in order to make a proper selection. A reliable BOLI consultant is an independent broker, a specialist who works for banks, not insurance companies. However, there are consultants in the market who are not true brokers, but rather agents of insurance companies. As a result, they are biased in their recommendations about insurance products.

It is important to distinguish between independent consultants and insurance company agents. A BOLI consultant should be an experienced broker with access to a full range of products and a variety of carriers. Making the right choice is critical in order to get access to objective information and the best product lines, pricing components, and investment performance.

Of course, buyers adapt to the marketplace and expect to deal with sales tactics in certain situations. But in the BOLI market, buying from salespeople with vested interests can be avoided if a reliable consultant is at hand to act as an objective and resourceful guide.

THE CONSULTANT AS MEDIATOR

The role of a consultant is to build a communication bridge between a bank and an insurance company which will serve as a pathway for the flow of information among all parties in the transaction — the bank, the carrier, and the consultant. The skill of a BOLI consultant will determine how much and what kind of information is available, and how fast it can be obtained. Key to this role is a consultant's knowledge of carriers and their products.

An experienced consultant works with carriers to help them respond to changes in the market. A consultant advises insurance companies on how to update existing products, make pricing more competitive, develop new products, and add plan features which respond to market needs. A top notch firm is an innovator that designs new products. A consultant's design capabilities should be at least as good as, if not better than, the technical or creative capacities of carriers. A consultant's understanding of every BOLI component must be comprehensive.

THE CONSULTANT AS NEGOTIATOR

With an insider's knowledge about how carriers and products work, a consultant is well positioned to negotiate a BOLI transaction on behalf of a bank. This includes policy pricing, underwriting, insurable interest, contractual provisions, future product availability, and competitive performance in the short and long term.

THE CONSULTANT AS BOLI PLAN ADMINISTRATOR

After a BOLI plan is set up, a consultant can administer the policies, providing management services over the life of the plan. (The administration of BOLI is detailed in Chapter 8.) A BOLI program may continue 40 years or longer. A bank should select a qualified, experienced consultant with whom it can comfortably work over a long period of time.

In essence, a consultant is a bank's "plan insurance" for successful and timely delivery of the purchased product. The complexity of the transaction requires attention to intricate details, ensuring the carrier delivers a plan that conforms with previous agreements.

DIRECT PURCHASES

Occasionally, a prospective buyer may consider purchasing BOLI directly from an insurance company. Sometimes bank officials believe their institutions will benefit by eliminating a consultant's role.

Going direct is not necessarily a viable option with many insurance companies. Many carriers distribute their products only through consultants, preferring to be relieved of all tasks except delivering the best product. Insurance companies recognize that, more than just selling or placing a product, BOLI involves partnership. The best way they can participate successfully in a partnership is by working with experienced consultants.

Astute carriers also know that consultants can help them compete better in the market. That translates into better products for buyers.

A third reason carriers choose to work through consultants is to improve policy administration. A consultant will work with a carrier to service policies, acting as a check point for possible errors and oversights. A consultant ensures accuracy and provides superior long-term plan administration.

Still, some carriers have tried to market products directly to buyers. Their efforts have not met with much success because the product itself is only a part of a BOLI transaction. For companies that have tried to sell direct, the inexperience of their sales forces and home offices has translated into high marketing and sales costs that are ultimately passed on to buyers.

A survey of the market shows that no major BOLI plans have been transacted on a direct basis. The most prudent banks select a top-rated consultant group to work with. Going direct can mean sacrificing competitive position, negotiating leverage, and long-term plan performance.

Lower Cost: Retail vs. Wholesale

All the same, some buyers believe it may be cheaper to buy BOLI direct from carriers. They believe a better deal can be had if they cut out the middleman, the broker/consultant, and buy wholesale, directly from the carrier.

Product placement represents a cost that carriers build into policy expense loads. One way or another, a carrier will seek to recover the expense. Product administration is another expense that carriers build into policy loads. These costs do not disappear when a consultant is eliminated. Depending on experience and internal administration, a consultant performs these services more efficiently and accurately than a carrier.

The carriers in the BOLI market are AAA and AA+ rated with billion dollar asset bases. Their financial position and claims-paying ability are based on their success in investing prudently. An insurance company's business is to minimize risk, cover its expenses, create profits, and maintain or increase its ratings. As single customers, most banks have neither the knowledge nor influence to negotiate the best margins in a direct purchase.

WHAT TO LOOK FOR IN A CONSULTANT

The role of a consultant is to put together the most profitable and financially sound BOLI program possible. A consultant should be selected with care since a bank will work with the firm for years to come.

Criteria for selecting a BOLI consultant include:

- Experience in the market
- Management stability
- Product availability
- In-house administrative capability and technical resources
- Design capability
- Impartiality

A buyer should evaluate a consultant informally through meetings and references, and formally through a "Request for Proposal."

Experience and Stability

Experience is a function of how long a company has been in business and the growth of its client base and support staff. A buyer should look for evidence that a consultant is willing to grow and change as the market changes.

A bank should ensure that a consultant has specific expertise in BOLI. There are many different focuses in the life insurance industry. A successful consultant in individual sales and personal financial planning would be ill-equipped to help a bank carry out a large life insurance purchase. A consultant's capabilities are demonstrated by its track record with carriers and clients.

A consultant must also understand the regulatory environment, taking into account rules enforced by a variety of public agencies and adhering to legal and insurance company guidelines on insurable interest. A well-regarded BOLI consultant may help official agencies to develop guidelines and tools of analysis.

Stability and staying power are essential in a consulting firm. As it implements a BOLI plan, a bank invests time and resources building a relationship with its consultant. This investment should be protected by working only with a consulting firm that is likely to be around for a long time.

A consulting firm should have a realistic succession plan in case key personnel leave. If a firm is built around one or two individuals whose leadership is essential for continuing the business, a bank could be vulnerable. A responsible consulting firm thinks and acts for the long term.

A consulting firm must also have adequate financial resources. Profitability helps ensure a firm's staying power if profits are reinvested in the business to develop resources, recruit and train top talent, and provide state-of-the-art tools. Such investments are evidence that a firm is planning to be around for a long time.

A client may ask to see a consulting firm's audited financial statements. Such statements show whether a firm is well capitalized or straining under a heavy debt burden.

Product Availability

There are more buyers than ready and willing suppliers in the BOLI market. As a result, product availability does not meet demand and requires negotiation with carriers. In some instances, product may be reserved for certain consultants based on the ability of those firms to place product quickly and to complete financially-sound transactions. A top-notch consulting firm not only seeks out products for buyers, but also uses its own resources to design new products for the market. A firm's ability to innovate establishes it as a leading-edge consultant from the viewpoint of carriers and prospective buyers.

Administrative Capabilities

The administrative capabilities of a firm are vital to the long-term success of a BOLI plan. The administrative services a firm provides and the data systems it maintains are important buyer concerns. A consultant should not rely on carriers for reporting functions, but should work independently to provide accurate, high-quality information to clients. Administrative calendars should be tailored to banks' reporting needs. Responsiveness and timeliness go hand-in-hand with accuracy.

A consultant's administrative abilities can be checked by determining the number of policies the firm has under administration and obtaining references from other clients across such disciplines as finance and human resources. The best way to learn whether a consultant is a good administrator is to visit the firm's administrative facility and meet staff people who will work with the BOLI plan on a daily basis.

In-house Resources

A quality firm should be able to offer clients the services of staff attorneys, accountants, actuaries, product designers, benefit experts, and communication specialists.

Design Capabilities

Product knowledge is an absolute essential in a consultant. A consultant should be prepared to custom design products and tailor plan features to meet a bank's specific needs.

Impartiality

Only an impartial firm can truly serve a bank as a partner. Some consultants have entered into arrangements with carriers in which they receive a share of profits from business they place for the carrier. This type of arrangement is not disclosed to the buyer, but can represent a significant part of a broker's income. Such hidden compensation is not an acceptable payment arrangement, as it violates industry standards and good business practice.

PARTNERING FOR SUCCESS

An impartial and objective consultant will help a bank develop a BOLI plan that properly serves all parties, meeting the financial criteria of the buyer, providing fair compensation to the consultant, and profitable business to the insurance company.

By carefully selecting a BOLI consultant, a bank can lay the foundation for a successful plan. Bank officials should seek a consulting firm they trust and with which they can work comfortably.

APPENDICES

APPENDIX A
OCC BANKING
CIRCULAR 249 (REV.)

Comptroller of the Currency
Administrator of National Banks

Type: Banking Circular

Subject: Bank Purchases of Life Insurance

To: Chief Executive Officers of all National Banks, Department and Division Heads, and all Examining Personnel

PURPOSE

This circular provides general guidelines for national banks to use in determining whether they may legally purchase a particular life insurance product.

BACKGROUND

In the past, bank purchases of term life insurance and traditional forms of permanent life insurance have raised few legal questions or supervisory concerns. Recently, however, the OCC has become concerned about bank purchases of insurance products with a significant investment component, such as single premium life insurance. In some cases, those purchases have raised serious questions about whether the bank has made an illegal investment in the cash surrender value (CSV) of life insurance. The OCC is also concerned because the unsecured cash surrender value of these policies has sometimes constituted a significant percentage of the bank's capital.

LEGAL AUTHORITY FOR PURCHASING LIFE INSURANCE

The authority for national banks to purchase and hold an interest in life insurance is found in 12 U.S.C. § 24(7). The law provides that national banks may exercise "all such incidental powers as shall be necessary to carry on the business of banking." The OCC has further delineated the scope of that authority through regulations, interpretive rulings, and letters addressing the use of life insurance for purposes incidental to banking. Those purposes include: key-person insurance, life insurance on borrowers, life insurance purchased in connection with employee compensation and benefit plans, and life insurance taken as security for loans. There is no authority under 12 U.S.C. § 24(7) for national banks to purchase life insurance for their own account as an investment.

POLICY GUIDELINES

A national bank may purchase or take an interest in life insurance for a purpose incidental to the business of banking. The amount of such insurance must closely approximate the bank's risk of loss or obligation arising from its relationship with the insured. National banks may not purchase life insurance as an investment.

A life insurance policy will be considered to be purchased and held for non-investment purposes if it satisfies either of the following tests:

Date: May 9, 1991   B2   Page 2 of 8 Pages

(A) When the bank purchases life insurance to indemnify itself against the death of an individual (as in the case of key-person insurance or insurance purchased on a borrower), the amount of insurance coverage must closely approximate the risk of loss. For purposes of measuring insurance coverage, the OCC considers the amount of insurance to be the total death benefit to be received upon the death of the insured. This includes the face amount of the policy, any premium to be returned, and accrued interest and/or dividends.

or

(B) When the bank purchases life insurance in conjunction with providing employee compensation or benefits, or when the insurance constitutes all or part of the benefit (as in so-called "split dollar" or other life insurance plans), the following condition must be satisfied:

Based upon reasonable actuarial benefit and financial assumptions, the present value of the projected cash flow from the policy must not substantially exceed the present value of the projected cost of the associated compensation or benefit program liabilities. The bank may include the insurance premiums paid and the associated time value of money in its calculation of the total cost of the liabilities.

The following sections provide more detailed guidance on the specific purposes for which national banks may purchase life insurance.

Date: May 9, 1991   B3   Page 3 of 8 Pages

KEY-PERSON INSURANCE

Interpretive Ruling 7.7115 (Insuring lives of bank officers), 12 C.F.R. § 7.7115, addresses those situations in which a national bank may obtain life insurance to protect itself against the loss of "key persons" in bank management. The ruling allows a national bank to purchase insurance on the life of an officer whose death would be of such consequence to the bank as to give it an insurable interest in his or her life. Interpretive letters have expanded the scope of this ruling to recognize the possibility that certain directors of the bank may also be key persons.

Key-person insurance must comply with non-investment test (A) of these guidelines. The bank's board of directors must adequately document the basis on which it determines an officer or director to be a key person. Similarly, the board of directors must adequately document the basis for determining the amount of insurance needed to indemnify the bank against the death of each key person. Interpretive Ruling 7.7115 does not authorize the purchase of life insurance on an individual who is not demonstrably a key-person. Nor does the Ruling permit the purchase of life insurance in an amount that is not reasonably related to the bank's potential loss.

The bank's authority to hold life insurance on a key person lapses if the individual, because of retirement, resignation, discharge, change of responsibilities or for any other reason, is no longer a key person for the bank. The desire to obtain the return of the premium paid, interest, or dividends on the policy does not provide an independent basis under 12 U.S.C. § 24(7) and Interpretive Ruling 7.7115 for retaining life insurance on an individual who no longer qualifies as a key person. Therefore, the economic consequences of terminating the insurance, or the ability to transfer the coverage to

Date: May 9, 1991   B4   Page 4 of 8 Pages

another key person, should be considerations in selecting a key-person insurance policy.

LIFE INSURANCE ON BORROWERS

State law generally recognizes that a lender has an insurable interest in the life of a borrower to the extent of the borrower's obligation to the lender. Interpretive Rulings 7.7495 (Debt cancellation contracts), 12 CFR § 7.7495, and 12 CFR § 2.6(c) and (f) (Methods of selling credit life insurance) are relevant for national banks. They recognize that national banks may protect themselves against the risk of loss from the death of a borrower. That protection may be provided through self-insurance in the form of debt cancellation contracts, or by the purchase of life insurance policies on borrowers.

Life insurance purchased on borrowers must comply with non-investment test (A) of these guidelines. For borrowers who are in good standing, a bank's potential loss is generally the principal balance of the borrower's obligations to the bank, including the maximum amount that could be borrowed under a line of credit, at the time the insurance is purchased. That amount would, therefore, be the maximum insurance coverage the bank could purchase on the borrower.

The purchase of life insurance on a borrower is not an appropriate mechanism for effecting a recovery on obligations that have been (or are expected to be) charged-off. Such life insurance purchases are not incidental to banking within the meaning of 12 U.S.C. § 24(7) because the insurance does not protect the bank against a risk of loss. In the case of charged-off loans, the bank has already realized the loss, and the purchase of life insurance more closely resembles an investment to recover on that loss.

LIFE INSURANCE PURCHASED IN CONNECTION WITH COMPENSATION AGREEMENTS AND BENEFIT PLANS

Under 12 U.S.C. § 24(5) and 12 CFR § 7.5220, national banks may enter into employment agreements with their officers and employees upon reasonable terms and conditions. It is the responsibility of the board of directors to establish and be able to justify the reasonableness of the compensation provided to bank employees under these agreements.

A national bank may provide life insurance benefits to its employees through individual or group policies for which the bank pays all or part of the premium. A national bank also may provide deferred compensation and retirement programs for bank employees. Similarly, a national bank may establish programs that permit directors to defer payment of all or a portion of their director fees.

Interpretive letters have established that a national bank may protect itself against its contractual obligations under such agreements through the purchase of life insurance. However, except as part of a reasonable compensation agreement or benefit plan, a national bank may not purchase life insurance as an estate management device for the benefit of officers, directors, or employees who are also controlling shareholders of the bank.

Life insurance purchased in connection with compensation agreements and benefit plans must comply with non-investment test (B) of these guidelines. Such policies may be held for as long as the bank continues to have any liability under the compensation or benefit plans for which the policies were initially purchased. A bank may, therefore, purchase insurance on a group of persons and continue to hold the insurance as long as it has any liability under the associated compensation or benefit plan.

LIFE INSURANCE AS SECURITY FOR LOANS

National banks may take an interest in an existing life insurance policy as security for a loan. National banks may also make loans to individuals for the purpose of purchasing life insurance, taking a security interest in the insurance policy. As with any other type of lending, extensions of credit secured by life insurance must be made on terms that are consistent with safe and sound banking principles. For instance, the borrower must be obligated to repay the loan according to an appropriate amortization schedule.

Generally, a national bank may not rely on its security interest in a life insurance policy to extend credit on terms that excuse the borrower from making interest and principal payments during the life of the borrower with the result that the bank is repaid only when the policy matures at the death of the insured. Lending on such terms may be treated as an illegal investment in life insurance under 12 U.S.C. § 24(7) since the bank would be looking to the life insurance benefits as its sole return on the funds it advanced.

OTHER CONSIDERATIONS

Life insurance death benefits and cash surrender values are unsecured obligations of the insurance company. Cash surrender value of insurance should be reported as an "Other asset" on the bank's financial statements.

Before purchasing a life insurance policy, the bank should evaluate the financial condition of the insurance company and continue to monitor its condition on an ongoing basis. The bank should consider the effect of any significant holdings of this ordinarily long-term asset on the bank's capital and liquidity. It should also determine the tax and other economic consequences of surrendering the insurance before the death of the insured should that become necessary.

APPLICATION OF THE GUIDELINES

Examiners will evaluate all current holdings and future purchases of life insurance by national banks in light of the guidelines in this circular.

ORIGINATING OFFICE

Questions about this circular should be directed to the Office of the Chief National Bank Examiner.

Donald G. Coonley
Chief National Bank Examiner

APPENDIX B

No. 010/November 14, 1985

FINANCIAL ACCOUNTING SERIES

FASB TECHNICAL BULLETIN No. 85-4

Title: *Accounting for Purchases of Life Insurance*

References:

- AICPA Accounting Interpretation, "Accounting for Key-Man Life Insurance"
- FASB Concepts Statement No. 3, *Elements of Financial Statements of Business Enterprises,* paragraphs 19 and 123

Question

1. How should an entity[1] account for an investment in life insurance?

Response

2. The amount that could be realized under the insurance contract as of the date of the statement of financial position should be reported as an asset. The change in cash surrender or contract value during the period is an adjustment of premiums paid in determining the expense or income to be recognized under the contract for the period.

---

[1]The provisions of this Technical Bulletin apply to all entities that purchase life insurance in which the entity is either the owner or beneficiary of the contract, without regard to the funding objective of the purchase. Such purchases would typically include those intended to meet loan covenants or to fund deferred compensation agreements, buy-sell agreements, or postemployment death benefits. Purchases of life insurance by retirement plans that are subject to FASB Statement No. 35 *Accounting and Reporting by Defined Benefit Pension Plans,* are not addressed by this Technical Bulletin.

Effective Date and Transition

3. The provisions of this Technical Bulletin are effective for insurance policies acquired after November 14, 1985.

Appendix

BACKGROUND

4. In November 1970, the AICPA issued an Accounting Interpretation entitled "Accounting for Key-Man Life Insurance." That Accounting Interpretation identified the cash surrender value method as generally accepted accounting for purchases of life insurance. New types of life insurance contracts, new provisions in traditional contracts, and changes in the insurance industry have led some to question the 1970 Accounting Interpretation. In October 1984, the AICPA's Accounting Standards Executive Committee (AcSEC) approved an Issues Paper entitled "Accounting for Key-Person Life Insurance." In the Issues Paper, AcSEC reaffirmed support

of the cash surrender value method as the only generally accepted method. The AcSEC position differed from the position of the AICPA Insurance Companies Committee, which supported use of a different method in certain circumstances. AcSEC was concerned that diversity would develop in practice because of the difference between those positions and requested that the FASB consider the matter.

5. A premium paid by a purchaser of life insurance serves a variety of purposes. A portion of the premium pays the insurer for assumption of mortality risk and provides for recovery of the insurer's contract acquisition, initiation, and maintenance costs. Another portion of the premium contributes to the accumulation of contract values. The relative amounts of premium payment credited to various contract attributes change over time as the age of the insured party increases and as earnings are credited to previously established contract values.

6. An insurance contract is significantly different from most investment agreements. The various attributes of the policy could be obtained separately through term insurance and purchase of investments. The combination of benefits and contract values could not, however, typically be acquired absent the insurance contract. Continued protection from mortality risk and realization of scheduled increases in contract accumulation usually requires payment of future premiums.

7. The payment of insurance premiums may take a number of different forms. The insurance contract may be purchased through payment of a single premium, as opposed to the typical series of future premiums. Alternatively, the premium payments may be made through loans from the insurance company that are secured by policy cash surrender values. The pattern of premium payments is a decision that

does not alter the underlying nature of the insurance contract.

Consideration of Comments Received on Proposed Technical Bulletin

8. A proposed Technical Bulletin, *Accounting for Business-Owned Life Insurance,* was released for comment on June 28, 1985. Forty-seven letters of comment were received on the proposed Technical Bulletin. Certain of the comments received and consideration of them are discussed in the following paragraphs.

9. Some respondents view the dominant objective of a life insurance contract to be investment. Subject to certain criteria evidencing an intent to continue the contract, they maintain that the contract meets the definition of an asset established in paragraph 19 of Concepts Statement 3, which states, "Assets are probable future economic benefits obtained or controlled by a particular entity as a result of past transactions or events" (footnote reference omitted). Those who hold this view suggested that such contracts should be accounted for using methods that result in reporting the investment in life insurance at amounts different from those stipulated in the contract.

10. This Technical Bulletin does not take that view. The current capacity to realize contract benefits is limited to settlement amounts specified in the contract. Additional amounts in excess of cash surrender value, which would be reported as assets under the various alternative accounting methods suggested, are created by future events, which typically include premium payments and earnings credited to contract amounts.

11. Paragraph 123 of Concepts Statement 3 discusses the occurrence of past events and the role of future events in the recognition of assets.

> Since the transaction or event giving rise to the enterprise's right to the future economic benefit must already have occurred, the definition excludes from assets items that may in the future become an enterprise's assets but have not yet become its assets. An enterprise has no asset for a particular future economic benefit if the transactions or events that give it access to and control of the benefit are yet in the future.

12. Some respondents asserted that reporting an insurance investment at its realizable value represents an accounting based on liquidation values. Those respondents suggested that the entity acquiring an insurance contract is, in many cases, economically or contractually committed to maintain the contract in force. They maintained that such a commitment virtually assures that benefits in excess of premiums paid would be realized and that the policy should be reported on a basis other than its cash surrender value.

13. This Technical Bulletin does not accept that view. The amount realizable under an insurance investment represents settlement values agreed to by an independent buyer and seller. The variety of yields and contract accumulation patterns available in the insurance marketplace provides the buyer and seller a variety of insurance and settlement options. There is no compelling justification to depart from the recording of such contracts based on agreed provisions. The commitment referred to by respondents is, in the staff's view, a commitment to ensure that assets are available to meet contractual obligations. The presence of such a commitment

does not change the measurement of the asset that is expected to satisfy the obligation.

14. Some respondents asserted that policy features, most notably the business exchange rider, were significant factors in determining the proper accounting for the policy. The business exchange rider allows a company to use values in an existing policy to insure a different employee when the originally insured employee leaves the company. They maintain that this feature gives the employer the ability to transfer the contract freely and enhances the employer's ability to realize the future value of the investment. They further maintain that the increased probability of realizing future values should lead to the reporting of amounts in excess of cash surrender value.

15. This Technical Bulletin rejects that view. The business exchange rider is a significant development in the design of business insurance products and reduces additional policy costs if a covered employee leaves the company. Such a provision does not affect the realization of future benefits under the insurance contract, nor does it change the traditional underwriting decisions involved in insuring a new life. Instead, the provision only reduces the cost of obtaining those benefits by allowing a new employee to be insured without the costs that are typically associated with obtaining a new policy.

APPENDIX C

The Federal Reserve, Comptroller of the Currency and Federal Deposit Insurance Commission have adopted risk-based capital guidelines to help evaluate and regulate banks and bank holding companies. The Office of Thrift Supervision has adopted similar guidelines for savings banks. All financial institutions are now familiar with the Tier 1, Tier 2 and leveraged ratios that must be calculated. The intent of this regulation is to create a profile which shows the risk factor in balance sheet assets and off balance sheet commitments. BOLI has a balance sheet presence and will have an impact on capital adequacy ratios. The significance of this impact depends on the assets the financial organization uses to purchase its BOLI plan. The table on page 126 outlines the various risk category and weights for bank assets.

Off balance sheet risks are included through equivalents, again depending on the appropriate risk weight classification.

When a financial institution sells a U.S. Treasury Bond in order to generate resources to purchase a BOLI plan, it is also moving this resource from a risk weight of 0% to a risk weight of 100%. Alternatively, if the bank asset sold is an agency bond or Collateralized Mortgage Obligation (CMO), the impact on capital adequacy would be less than using cash or a U.S. Treasury because of the weighting differential. An example of how BOLI will impact Capital Adequacy (in millions) is on page 127.

VARIOUS RISK CATEGORY AND WEIGHTS FOR BANK ASSETS		
Risk Category	Definition	Risk Weighting
1	Cash and direct debt of the U.S. government and its agencies	0%
2	Claims on domestic depository institutions, debt unconditionally guaranteed by the U.S. government, and debt of government-sponsored agencies	20%
3	Accruing loans secured by first liens on one-to-four family residences, mortgaged-backed securities backed by conventional mortgages and certain state or local revenue bonds or revenue-backed obligations.	50%
4	All other Assets (Including BOLI)	100%

CAPITAL ADEQUACY BALANCE SHEET
(IN MILLIONS)

		Risk Category			
		0%	20%	50%	100%
U.S. Treasuries	$ 2,000	$ 2,000			
U.S. Agencies	$ 750		$ 750		
Residential Real Estate Loans	$ 3,000			$ 3,000	
Other Loans	$ 7,000				$ 7,000
Other Assets	$ 400				$ 400
Total Assets	$13,150				
Risk Weighted Assets		0 +	$ 150 +	$ 1,500 +	$ 7,400

Total Risk Weighted Assets .... $ 9,050

	Tier 1		Tier 2		
Shareholders' Equity	$ 950				
Capital Notes			$ 150		
Loan Reserve			$ 110		
Total	$ 950	+	$ 260	=	$ 1,210

EFFECT OF BOLI INVESTMENT ON CAPITAL RATIO

(refer to page 127)

	Tier 1 *(Regulatory Minimum 4.0%)*	Tier 1 plus 2 *(Regulatory Minimum 8.0%)*
*Pre-BOLI Investment Capital Ratio ***	10.50%	13.37%
Post-BOLI Investment Capital Ratio		
Scenario 1: Sells U.S. Treasury bond to invest $200 million in BOLI	10.27%	13.08%
Scenario 2: Sells a CMO to invest $200 million in BOLI	10.38%	13.22%

*Capital as a percentage of risk-weighted assets.

APPENDIX D

Sample Bank CONSOLIDATED INCOME STATEMENT $100,000,000 PURCHASE ILLUSTRATION			
	(in thousands, except per share data)		
	1994	Pro Forma	Change
Interest Income			
Interest and Fees on Loans and Leases	$ 735,530		
Interest on Securities			
Taxable	169,316	163,236	(6,080) [1]
Exempt from Income Taxes	16,436		
Total Interest on Securities	185,752		
Interest on Other Short-Term Investments	1,019		
Total Interest Income	922,301	916,221	(6,080)
Interest Expense			
Interest on Deposits			
Interest Checking	25,572		
Savings	14,511		
Money Market	40,326		
Other Time	194,375		
Certificates-$100,000 and Over	13,135		
Foreign Office	24,165		
Total Interest on Deposits	312,084		
Interest on Federal Funds Borrowed	34,925		
Interest on Short-Term Bank Notes	20,285		
Interest on Other Short-Term Borrowings	25,818		
Interest on Long-Term Debt and Notes	12,436		
Total Interest Expense	405,548	405,548	-
Net Interest Income	516,753	510,673	(6,080)
Provision for Credit Losses	35,780	35,780	-
Net Interest Income After Provision for Credit Losses	480,973	474,893	(6,080)
Other Operating Income			
Trust Income	55,238		
Service Charges on Deposits	60,905		
Data Processing Income	64,394		
Other Service Charges and Fees	74,978	80,878	5,900 [2]
Securities Gains	393		
Total Other Operating Income	255,908	261,808	5,900
Operating Expenses			
Salaries and Wages	144,513		
Employee Benefits	36,710		
Equipment Expenses	16,045		
Net Occupancy Expenses	26,137		
Other Operating Expenses	148,140		
Total Operating Expenses	371,545	371,545	-
Income Before Income Taxes	365,336	365,156	(180)
Applicable Income Taxes	120,877	118,749	(2,128) [3]
Net Income	$ 244,459	$246,407	$ 1,948
Net Income Per Share	$ 3.80	$ 3.83	$ 0.03

See following page for Assumptions and Footnotes to Pro Forma

ASSUMPTIONS

- Sell $100 million in Agency mortage-backed securities (one to five year maturity) with an estimated annual yield of 6.08%.
- Buy $100 million of BOLI (PEP) with an annual yield of 5.9%.
- Sample Bank's Federal tax rate is 35%.

FOOTNOTES TO PRO FORMA

[1] The interest income that the bank earned on $100 million in Agency mortgage-backed securities at 6.08% (i.e., $6.08 million) is reversed out of the amount of existing taxable securities interest income.

[2] Income generated by a $100 million purchase of BOLI is $5.9 million.

[3] Reduced interest income for the taxable securities also results in a reduced tax. Using a 35% tax rate, eliminating $6.08 million of taxable interest income results in a tax savings of $2.13 million.

ESTIMATED VALUE OF
BANK OWNED LIFE INSURANCE
TO THE SHAREHOLDERS OF [SAMPLE BANK]

	1994	With BOLI In 1994	Change
Stock Price	$48.00	$48.38	$0.38
Net Income	$244,449,000	$246,397,000	$1,948,000
EPS	$3.80	$3.83	$0.03
P/E Ratio	12.63	12.63	------
Market Value: Per Share	$48.00	$48.38	$0.38
Market Value: Aggregate	$3,087,776,842	$3,112,383,158	$24,606,316

This illustration is based on a $100 million BOLI transaction.

APPENDIX E

INTERNAL REVENUE CODE
1986 CODE–SUBTITLE A, CH. 1B, PART IX
SEC. 264. CERTAIN AMOUNTS PAID IN
CONNECTION WITH INSURANCE CONTRACTS.

[Sec. 264(a)]

(a) GENERAL RULE.–No deduction shall be allowed for–

(1) Premiums paid on any life insurance policy covering the life of any officer or employee, or of any person financially interested in any trade or business carried on by the taxpayer, when the taxpayer is directly or indirectly a beneficiary under such policy.

(2) Any amount paid or accrued on indebtedness incurred or continued to purchase or carry a single premium life insurance, endowment, or annuity contract.

(3) Except as provided in subsection (c), any amount paid or accrued on indebtedness incurred or continued to purchase or carry a life insurance, endowment, or annuity contract (other than a single premium contract or a contract treated as a single premium contract) pursuant to a plan of purchase which contemplates the systematic direct or indirect borrowing of part or all of the increases in the cash value of such contract (either from the insurer or otherwise).

(4) Any interest paid or accrued on any indebtedness with respect to 1 or more life insurance policies owned by the taxpayer covering the life of any individual who—

(A) is an officer or employee of, or

(B) is financially interested in,

any trade or business carried on by the taxpayer to the extent that the aggregate amount of such indebtedness with respect to policies covering such individual exceeds $50,000.

Paragraph (2) shall apply in respect of annuity contracts only as to contracts purchased after March 1, 1954. Paragraph (3) shall apply only in respect of contracts purchased after August 6, 1963. Paragraph (4) shall apply with respect to contracts purchased after June 20, 1986.

Amendments

P.L. 99-514, § 1003(a):

Act Sec. 1003(a) amended Code Sec. 264(a) by adding after paragraph (3) new paragraph (4) to read as above.

The above amendment applies to contracts purchased after June 20, 1986, in tax years ending after such date.

P.L. 99-514, § 1003(b):

Act Sec. 1003(b) amended Code Sec. 264(a) by adding a new sentence at the end thereof to read as above.

The above amendment applies to contracts purchased after June 20, 1986, in tax years ending after such date.

P.L. 88-272, § 215(a):

Amended subsection (a) to add paragraph (3) and to add at the end of subsection (a) the last sentence. The amendment applies with respect to contracts purchased after August 6, 1963.

[Sec. 264(b)]

(b) CONTRACTS TREATED AS SINGLE PREMIUM CONTRACTS.—For purposes of subsection (a) (2), a contract shall be treated as a single premium contract—

> (1) if substantially all the premiums on the contract are paid within a period of 4 years from the date on which the contract is purchased, or

> (2) if an amount is deposited after March 1, 1954, with the insurer for payment of a substantial number of future premiums on the contract.

[Sec. 264(c)]

(c) EXCEPTIONS.—Subsection (a)(3) shall not apply to any amount paid or accrued by a person during a taxable year on indebtedness incurred or continued as part of a plan referred to in subsection (a)(3)—

> (1) if no part of 4 of the annual premiums due during the 7-year period (beginning with the date the first premium on the contract to which such plan relates was paid) is paid under such plan by means of indebtedness,

> (2) if the total of the amounts paid or accrued by such person during such taxable year for which (without regard to this paragraph) no deduction would be allowable by reason of subsection (a)(3) does not exceed $100,

> (3) if such amount was paid or accrued on indebtedness incurred because of an unforeseen substantial loss of income or unforeseen substantial increase in his financial obligations, or

(4) if such indebtedness was incurred in connection with his trade or business.

For purposes of applying paragraph (1), if there is a substantial increase in the premiums on a contract, a new 7-year period described in such paragraph with respect to such contract shall commence on the date the first such increased premium is paid.

Amendments

P.L. 88-272, § 215(b):

Amended section 264 to add subsection (c) above. The amendment applies with respect to amounts paid or accrued in taxable years beginning after December 31, 1963.

APPENDIX F

INTERNAL REVENUE CODE
1986 CODE-SUBTITLE F, CH. 79

Definitions

[Sec. 7702]

SEC. 7702. LIFE INSURANCE CONTRACT DEFINED.

[Sec. 7702(a)]

(a) GENERAL RULE.–For purposes of this title, the term "life insurance contract" means any contract which is a life insurance contract under the applicable law, but only if such contract–

(1) meets the cash value accumulation test of subsection (b), or

(2)(A) meets the guideline premium requirements of subsection (c), and

(B) falls within the cash value corridor of subsection (d).

[Sec. 7702(b)]

(b) CASH VALUE ACCUMULATION TEST FOR SUBSECTION (a)(1).–

(1) IN GENERAL.–A contract meets the cash value accumulation test of this subsection if, by the terms of the contract, the cash surrender value of such contract may not at any time exceed the net single premium which would have to be paid at such time to fund future benefits under the contract.

(2) RULES FOR APPLYING PARAGRAPH (1).–Determinations under paragraph (1) shall be made–

(A) on the basis of interest at the greater of an annual effective rate of 4 percent or the rate or rates guaranteed on issuance of the contract,

(B) on the basis of the rules of subparagraph (B)(i) (and, in the case of qualified additional benefits, subparagraph (B)(ii)) of subsection (c)(3), and

(C) by taking into account under subparagraphs (A) and (D) of subsection (e)(1) only current and future death benefits and qualified additional benefits.

Amendments

P.L. 99-514, § 1825(a)(2):

Act Sec. 1825(a)(2) amended Code Sec. 7702(b)(2)(C) by striking out "subparagraphs (A) and (C)" and inserting in lieu thereof "subparagraphs (A) and (D)".

The above amendment is effective as if included in the provisions of P.L. 98-369 to which such amendment relates.

[Sec. 7702(c)]

(c) GUIDELINE PREMIUM REQUIREMENTS.–For purposes of this section-

(1) IN GENERAL.–A contract meets the guideline premium requirements of this subsection if the sum of the premiums paid under such contract does not at any time exceed the guideline premium limitation as of such time.

(2) GUIDELINE PREMIUM LIMITATION.–The term "guideline premium limitation" means, as of any date, the greater of–

(A) the guideline single premium, or

(B) the sum of the guideline level premiums to such date.

(3) GUIDELINE SINGLE PREMIUM.–

(A) IN GENERAL.–The term "guideline single premium" means the premium at issue with respect to future benefits under the contract.

(B) BASIS ON WHICH DETERMINATION IS MADE.–The determination under subparagraph (A) shall be based on–

(i) reasonable mortality charges which meet the requirements (if any) prescribed in regulations and which (except as provided in regulations) do not exceed the mortality charges specified in the prevailing commissioners' standard tables (as defined in section 807(d)(5)) as of the time the contract is issued,

(ii) any reasonable charges (other than mortality charges) which (on the basis of the company's experience, if any, with respect to similar contracts) are reasonably expected to be actually paid, and

(iii) interest at the greater of an annual effective rate of 6 percent or the rate or rates guaranteed on issuance of the contract.

(C) WHEN DETERMINATION MADE.—
Except as provided in subsection (f)(7), the determination under subparagraph (A) shall be
made as of the time the contract is issued.

(D) SPECIAL RULES FOR SUBPARAGRAPH
(B)(ii).–

(i) CHARGES NOT SPECIFIED IN THE
CONTRACT.–If any charge is not specified in
the contract, the amount taken into account
under subparagraph (B)(ii) for such charge
shall be zero.

(ii) NEW COMPANIES, ETC.–If any company
does not have adequate experience for purposes of the determination under subparagraph
(B)(ii), to the extent provided in regulations,
such determination shall be made on the basis of the industry-wide experience.

(4) GUIDELINE LEVEL PREMIUM.–The term
"guideline level premium" means the level annual amount, payable over a period not ending
before the insured attains age 95, computed on
the same basis as the guideline single premium,
except that paragraph (3)(B)(iii) shall be applied
by substituting "4 percent" for "6 percent".

Amendments

P.L.100-647, § 5011(a):

Act Sec. 5011(a) amended Code Sec. 7702(c)(3)(B) by
striking out clauses (i) and (ii) and inserting in lieu thereof
new clauses (i) and (ii) to read as above. Prior to amendment, Code Sec. 7702(c)(3)(B)(i)-(ii) read as follows:

(i) the mortality charges specified in the contract (or, if none is specified, the mortality charges used in determining the statutory reserves for such contract),

(ii) any charges (not taken into account under clause (i)) specified in the contract (the amount of any charge not so specified shall be treated as zero), and

P.L. 100-647, § 5011(b):

Act Sec. 5011(b) amended Code Sec. 7702(c)(3) by adding at the end thereof a new subparagraph (D) to read as above.

The above amendments apply to contracts entered into on or after October 21, 1988.

[Sec. 7702(d)]

(d) CASH VALUE CORRIDOR FOR PURPOSES OF SUBSECTION (a)(2)(B).—For purposes of this section—

(1) IN GENERAL.–A contract falls within the cash value corridor of this subsection if the death benefit under the contract at any time is not less than the applicable percentage of the cash surrender value.

(2) APPLICABLE PERCENTAGE.– See following page for chart.

In the case of an insured with an attained age as of the beginning of the contract year of:

The applicable percentage shall decrease by a ratable portion for each full year:

More than:	But not more than:	From:	To:
0	40	250	250
40	45	250	215
45	50	215	185
50	55	185	150
55	60	150	130
60	65	130	120
65	70	120	115
70	75	115	105
75	90	105	105
90	95	105	100

[Sec. 7702(e)]

(e) COMPUTATIONAL RULES.–

(1) IN GENERAL.–For purposes of this section (other than subsection (d))–

(A) the death benefit (and any qualified additional benefit) shall be deemed not to increase,

(B) the maturity date, including the date on which any benefit described in subparagraph (C) is payable, shall be deemed to be no earlier than the day on which the insured attains age 95, and no later than the day on which the insured attains age 100,

(C) the death benefits shall be deemed to be provided until the maturity date determined by taking into account subparagraph (B), and

(D) the amount of any endowment benefit (or sum of endowment benefits, including any cash surrender value on the maturity date determined by taking into account subparagraph (B)) shall be deemed not to exceed the least amount payable as a death benefit at any time under the contract.

(2) LIMITED INCREASES IN DEATH BENEFIT PERMITTED.–Notwithstanding paragraph (1)(A)–

(A) for purposes of computing the guideline level premium, an increase in the death benefit which is provided in the contract may be taken into account but only to the extent necessary to prevent a decrease in the excess of the death benefit over the cash surrender value of the contract,

(B) for purposes of the cash value accumulation test, the increase described in subparagraph (A) may be taken into account if the contract will meet such test at all times assuming that the net level reserve (determined as if level annual premiums were paid for the contract over a period not ending before the insured attains age 95) is substituted for the net single premium,

(C) for purposes of the cash value accumulation test, the death benefit increases may be taken into account if the contract—

(i) has an initial death benefit of $5,000 or less and a maximum death benefit of $25,000 or less,

(ii) provides for a fixed predetermined annual increase not to exceed 10 percent of the initial death benefit or 8 percent of the death benefit at the end of the preceding year, and

(iii) was purchased to cover payment of burial expenses or in connection with prearranged funeral expenses.

For purposes of subparagraph (C), the initial death benefit of a contract shall be determined by treating all contracts issued to the same contract owner as 1 contract.

Amendments

P.L. 99-514 § 1825(a)(1)(A)-(D):

Act Sec. 1825(a)(1)(A)-(D) amended Code Sec. 7702(e)(1) by striking out "shall be no earlier than" in subparagraph (B) and inserting in lieu thereof "shall be deemed to be no earlier than", by striking out "and" at the end of subparagraph (B), by redesignating subparagraph (C) as subparagraph (D) and inserting after subparagraph (B) new subparagraph (C) to read as above, and by striking out "the maturity date described in subparagraph (B)" in subparagraph (D) (as so redesignated) and inserting in lieu thereof "the maturity date determined by taking into account subparagraph (B)".

The above amendment is effective as if included in the provisions of P.L. 98-369 to which such amendment relates.

P.L. 99-514, § 1825(a)(3):

Act Sec. 1825(a)(3) amended Code Sec. 7702(e)(1) by inserting "(other than subsection (d))" after "section".

The above amendment is effective as if included in the provisions of P.L. 98-369 to which such amendment relates.

P.L. 99-514, § 1825(a)(4)(A)-(C):

Act Sec. 1825(a)(4)(A)-(C) amended Code Sec. 7702(e)(2) by striking out "and" at the end of subparagraph (A), by striking out the period at the end of subparagraph (B), and inserting in lieu thereof a comma and "and", and by adding at the end thereof new subparagraph (C) to read as above.

The above amendment is effective with respect to contracts entered into after October 22, 1986 [effective date changed by P.L. 100-647, § 1018(j)].

[Sec. 7702(f)]

(f) OTHER DEFINITIONS AND SPECIAL RULES.–For purposes of this section–

(1) PREMIUMS PAID.–

(A) IN GENERAL.–The term "premiums paid" means the premiums paid under the contract less amounts (other than amounts includible in gross income) to which section 72(e) applies and less any excess premiums with respect to which there is a distribution described in sub-paragraph (B) or (E) of paragraph (7) and any other amounts received with respect to the contract which are specified in regulations.

(B) TREATMENT OF CERTAIN PREMIUMS RETURNED TO POLICYHOLDER.–If, in order to comply with the requirements of subsection (a)(2)(A), any portion of any premium paid during any contract year is returned by the insurance company (with interest) within 60 days after the end of a contract year, the amount so returned (excluding interest) shall be deemed to reduce the sum of the premiums paid under the contract during such year.

(C) INTEREST RETURNED INCLUDIBLE IN GROSS INCOME.–Notwithstanding the provisions of section 72(e), the amount of any interest returned as provided in subparagraph (B) shall be includible in the gross income of the recipient.

(2) CASH VALUES–

(A) CASH SURRENDER VALUE.–The cash surrender value of any contract shall be its cash value determined without regard to any surrender charge, policy loan, or reasonable termination dividends.

(B) NET SURRENDER VALUE.–The net surrender value of any contract shall be determined with regard to surrender charges but without regard to any policy loan.

(3) DEATH BENEFIT.–The term "death benefit" means the amount payable by reason of the death of the insured (determined without regard to any qualified additional benefits).

(4) FUTURE BENEFITS.–The term "future benefits" means death benefits and endowment benefits.

(5) QUALIFIED ADDITIONAL BENEFITS.–

(A) IN GENERAL.–The term "qualified additional benefits" means any–

(i) guaranteed insurability,

(ii) accidental death or disability benefit,

(iii) family term coverage,

(iv) disability waiver benefit, or

(v) other benefit prescribed under regulations.

(B) TREATMENT OF QUALIFIED ADDITIONAL BENEFITS.–For purposes of this section, qualified additional benefits shall not be treated as future benefits under the contract, but the charges for such benefits shall be treated as future benefits.

(C) TREATMENT OF OTHER ADDITIONAL BENEFITS.–In the case of any additional benefit which is not a qualified additional benefit–

(i) such benefit shall not be treated as a future benefit, and

(ii) any charge for such benefit which is not prefunded shall not be treated as a premium.

146

(6) PREMIUM PAYMENTS NOT DISQUALIFYING CONTRACT.–The payment of a premium which would result in the sum of the premiums paid exceeding the guideline premium limitation shall be disregarded for purposes of subsection (a)(2) if the amount of such premium does not exceed the amount necessary to prevent the termination of the contract on or before the end of the contract year (but only if the contract will have no cash surrender value at the end of such extension period).

(7) ADJUSTMENTS.–

(A) IN GENERAL.–If there is a change in the benefits under (or in other terms of) the contract which was not reflected in any previous determination or adjustment made under this section, there shall be proper adjustments in future determinations made under this section.

(B) RULE FOR CERTAIN CHANGES DURING FIRST 15 YEARS.–If–

(i) a change described in subparagraph (A) reduces benefits under the contract,

(ii) the change occurs during the 15-year period beginning on the issue date of the contract, and

(iii) a cash distribution is made to the policyholder as a result of such change,

section 72 (other than subsection (e)(5) thereof) shall apply to such cash distribution to the extent it does not exceed the recapture ceiling determined under subparagraph (C) or (D) (whichever applies).

(C) RECAPTURE CEILING WHERE CHANGE OCCURS DURING FIRST 5 YEARS.—If the change referred to in subparagraph (B)(ii) occurs during the 5-year period beginning on the issue date of the contract, the recapture ceiling is—

(i) in the case of a contract to which subsection (a)(1) applies, the excess of—

(I) the cash surrender value of the contract, immediately before the reduction, over

(II) the net single premium (determined under subsection (b)), immediately after the reduction, or

(ii) in the case of a contract to which subsection (a)(2) applies, the greater of—

(I) the excess of the aggregate premiums paid under the contract, immediately before the reduction, over the guideline premium limitation for the contract (determined under subsection (c)(2), taking into account the adjustment described in subparagraph (A)), or

(II) the excess of the cash surrender value of the contract, immediately before the reduction, over the cash value corridor of subsection (d) (determined immediately after the reduction).

(D) RECAPTURE CEILING WHERE CHANGE OCCURS AFTER 5TH YEAR AND BEFORE 16TH YEAR.–If the change referred to in sub-paragraph (B) occurs after the 5-year period referred to under subparagraph (C), the recapture ceiling is the excess of the cash surrender value of the contract, immediately before the reduction, over the cash value corridor of subsection (d) (determined immediately after the reduction and whether or not subsection (d) applies to the contract).

(E) TREATMENT OF CERTAIN DISTRIBUTIONS MADE IN ANTICIPATION OF BENEFIT REDUCTIONS.– Under regulations prescribed by the Secretary, subparagraph (B) shall apply also to any distribution made in anticipation of a re-duction in benefits under the contract. For purposes of the preceding sentence, appropri-ate adjustments shall be made in the provisions of subparagraphs (C) and (D); and any distri-bution which reduces the cash surrender value of a contract and which is made within 2 years before a reduction in benefits under the con-tract shall be treated as made in anticipation of such reduction.

(8) CORRECTION OF ERRORS.–If the taxpayer establishes to the satisfaction of the Secretary that–

(A) the requirements described in subsection (a) for any contract year were not satisfied due to reasonable error, and

(B) reasonable steps are being taken to remedy the error,

the Secretary may waive the failure to satisfy such requirements.

(9) SPECIAL RULE FOR VARIABLE LIFE INSURANCE CONTRACTS.–In the case of any contract which is a variable contract (as defined in section 817), the determination of whether such contract meets the requirements of subsection (a) shall be made whenever the death benefits under such contract change but not less frequently than once during each 12-month period.

Amendments

P.O. 99-514 § 1825(b)(1):

Act Sec. 1825(b)(1) amended Code Sec. 7702(f)(7) to read as above. Prior to amendment, Code Sec. 7702(f)(7) read as follows:

(7) ADJUSTMENTS.–

(A) IN GENERAL.–In the event of a change in the future benefits of any qualified additional benefit (or in any other terms) under the contract which was not reflected in any previous determination made under this section, under regulations prescribed by the Secretary, there shall be proper adjustments in future determinations made under this section.

(B) CERTAIN CHANGES TREATED AS EXCHANGE.–In the case of any change which reduces the future benefits under the contract, such change shall be treated as an exchange of the contract for another contract.

The above amendment is effective as if included in the provisions of P.L. 98-369 to which such amendment relates.

P.L. 99-514, § 1825(b)(2):

Act Sec. 1825(b)(2) amended Code Sec. 7702(f)(1)(A) by striking out "less any other amounts received" and inserting in lieu thereof "less any excess premiums with respect to which there is a distribution described in subparagraph (B) or (E) of paragraph (7) and any other amounts received".

The above amendment is effective as if included in the provisions of P.L. 98-369 to which such amendment relates.

[Sec. 7702(g)]

(g) TREATMENT OF CONTRACTS WHICH DO NOT MEET SUBSECTION (A) TEST.–

(1) INCOME INCLUSION.–

(A) IN GENERAL.–If at any time any contract which is a life insurance contract under the applicable law does not meet the definition of life insurance contract under subsection (a), the income on the contract for any taxable year of the policyholder shall be treated as ordinary income received or accrued by the policyholder during such year.

(B) INCOME ON THE CONTRACT.–For purposes of this paragraph, the term "income on the contract" means, with respect to any taxable year of the policyholder, the excess of–

(i) the sum of–

(I) the increase in the net surrender value of the contract during the taxable year, and

(II) the cost of life insurance protection provided under the contract during the taxable year, over

(ii) the premiums paid (as defined in subsection (f)(1)) under the contract during the taxable year.

(C) CONTRACTS WHICH CEASE TO MEET DEFINITION.–If, during any taxable year of the policyholder, a contract which is a life insurance contract under the applicable law ceases to meet the definition of life insurance contract under subsection (a), the income on the contract for all prior taxable years shall be treated as received or accrued during the taxable year in which such cessation occurs.

(D) COST OF LIFE INSURANCE PROTECTION.–For purposes of this paragraph, the cost of life insurance protection provided under the contract shall be the lesser of–

(i) the cost of individual insurance on the life of the insured as determined on the basis of uniform premiums (computed on the basis of 5-year age brackets) prescribed by the Secretary by regulations, or

(ii) the mortality charge (if any) stated in the contract.

(2) TREATMENT OF AMOUNT PAID ON DEATH OF INSURED.–If any contract which is

a life insurance contract under the applicable law does not meet the definition of life insurance contract under subsection (a), the excess of the amount paid by the reason of the death of the insured over the net surrender value of the contract shall be deemed to be paid under a life insurance contract for purposes of section 101 and subtitle B.

(3) CONTRACT CONTINUES TO BE TREATED AS INSURANCE CONTRACT.–If any contract which is a life insurance contract under the applicable law does not meet the definition of life insurance contract under subsection (a), such contract shall, notwithstanding such failure, be treated as an insurance contract for purposes of this title.

Amendments

P.L. 99-514, § 1825(c):

Act Sec. 1825(c) amended Code Sec. 7702(g)(1)(B)(ii) to read as above. Prior to amendment, Code Sec. 7702(g)(1)(B)(ii) read as follows:

> (ii) the amount of premiums paid under the contract during the taxable year reduced by policyholder dividends received during such taxable year.

The above amendment is effective as if included in the provisions of P.L. 98-369 to which such amendment relates.

[Sec. 7702(h)]

(h) ENDOWMENT CONTRACTS RECEIVE SAME TREATMENT.–

(1) IN GENERAL.–References in subsections (a) and (g) to a life insurance contract shall be treated as including references to a contract which is an endowment contract under the applicable law.

(2) DEFINITION OF ENDOWMENT CONTRACT.–For purposes of this title (other than paragraph (1)), the term "endowment contract" means a contract which is an endowment contract under the applicable law and which meets the requirements of subsection (a).

[Sec. 7702(i)]

(i) TRANSITIONAL RULE FOR CERTAIN 20-PAY CONTRACTS.–

(1) IN GENERAL.–In the case of a qualified 20-pay contract, this section shall be applied by substituting "3 percent" for "4 percent" in subsection (b)(2).

(2) QUALIFIED 20-PAY CONTRACT.–For purposes of paragraph (1), the term "qualified 20-pay contact" means any contract which–

(A) requires at least 20 nondecreasing annual premium payments, and

(B) is issued pursuant to an existing plan of insurance.

(3) EXISTING PLAN OF INSURANCE.–For purposes of this subsection, the term "existing plan of insurance" means, with respect to any contract, any plan of insurance which was filed by the company issuing such contract in 1 or

more States before September 28, 1983, and is on file in the appropriate State for such contract.

[Sec. 7702(j)]

(j) CERTAIN CHURCH SELF FUNDED DEATH BENEFIT PLANS TREATED AS LIFE INSURANCE.–

(1) IN GENERAL.–In determining whether any plan or arrangement described in paragraph (2) is a life insurance contract, the requirement of subsection (a) that the contract be a life insurance contract under applicable law shall not apply.

(2) DESCRIPTION.–For purposes of this subsection, a plan or arrangement is described in this paragraph if–

(A) such plan or arrangement provides for the payment of benefits by reason of the death of the individuals covered under such plan or arrangement, and

(B) such plan or arrangement is provided by a church for the benefit of its employees and their beneficiaries, directly or through an organization described in section 414(e)(3)(A) or an organization described in section 414(e)(3)(B)(ii).

(3) DEFINITIONS.–For purposes of this subsection–

(A) CHURCH.–The term "church" means a church or a convention or association of churches.

(B) EMPLOYEE.–The term "employee" includes an employee described in section (414)(e)(3)(B).

Amendments

P.L. 100-647, § 6078(a):

Act Sec. 6078(a) amended Code Sec. 7702 by inserting after subsection (i) new subsection (j) to read as above.

The above amendment is effective as if included in the amendments made by section 221(a) of the Tax Reform Act of 1984 (P.L. 98-369).

[Sec 7702(k)]

(k) REGULATIONS.— The Secretary shall prescribe such regulations as may be necessary or appropriate to carry out the purposes of this section.

Amendments

P.L. 100-647, § 6078(a):

Act Sec. 6078(a) amended Code Sec. 7702 by redesignating subsection (j) as subsection (k).

The above amendment is effective as if included in the amendments made by section 221(a) of the Tax Reform Act of 1984 (P.L. 98-369) to which it relates.

P.L. 98-369, § 221(a):

Act Sec. 221(a) added Code Sec. 7702, above.

The above amendment applies to contracts issued after December 31, 1984, in tax years ending after such date. Special rules appear below.

P.L. 98-369, § 221(d)(2)-(5), as amended by P.L. 99-514, § 1825(e):

(2) Special rule for certain contracts issued after June 30, 1984.—

(A) General Rule.–Except as otherwise provided in this paragraph, the amendments made by this section shall apply also to any contract issued after June 30, 1984, which provides an increasing death benefit and has premium funding more rapid than 10-year level premium payments.

(B) Exception for certain contracts.–– Subparagraph (A) shall not apply to any contract if–

(i) such contract (whether or not a flexible premium contract) would meet the requirements of section 101(f) of the Internal Revenue Code of 1954,

(ii) such contract is not a flexible premium life insurance contract (within the meaning of section 101(f) of such Code) and would meet the requirements of section 7702 of such Code determined by–

(I) substituting "3 percent" for "4 percent" in section 7702(b)(2) of such Code, and

(II) treating subparagraph (B) of section 7702(e)(1) of such Code as if it reads as follows: "the maturity date shall be the latest maturity date permitted under the contract, but not less than 20 years after the date of issue or (if earlier) age 95", or

(iii) under such contract–

(I) the premiums (including any policy fees) will be adjusted from time-to-time to reflect the level amount necessary (but not less than zero) at the time of such adjustment to provide a level death benefit assuming interest crediting and an annual effective interest rate of not less than 3 percent, or

(II) at the option of the insured, in lieu of an adjustment under subclause (I) there will be a comparable adjustment in the amount of the death benefit.

(C) Certain contracts issued before October 1, 1984.–

(i) In general.–Subparagraph (A) shall be applied by substituting "September 30, 1984" for "June 30, 1984" thereof in the case of a contract–

(I) which would meet the requirements of section 7702 of such Code if "3 percent" were substituted for "4 percent" in section 7702(b)(2) of such Code, and the rate or rates guaranteed on issuance of the contract were determined without regard to any mortality charges and any initial excess interest guarantees, and

(II) the cash surrender value of which does not at any time exceed the net single premium which would have to be paid at such time to fund future benefits under the contract.

(ii) Definitions.–For purposes of clause(i)–

(I) In general.–Except as provided in subclause (II), terms used in clause (i) shall have the same meanings as when used in section 7702 of such Code.

(II) Net single premium.–The term "net single premium" shall be determined by substituting "3 percent" for "4 percent" in section 7702(b)(2) of such Code, by using 1958 standard ordinary mortality and morbidity tables of the National Association of Insurance Commissioners, and by assuming a level death benefit.

(3) Transitional rule for certain existing plans of insurance.–A plan of insurance on file in 1 or more States before September 28, 1983, shall be treated for purposes of section 7702(i)(3) of such Code as a plan of insurance on file in 1 or more States before September 28, 1983, without regard to whether such plan of insurance is modified after September 28, 1983, to permit the crediting of excess interest or similar amounts annually and not monthly under contracts issued pursuant to such plan of insurance.

(4) Extension of flexible premium contract provisions.–The amendments made by subsection (b) shall take effect on January 1, 1984.

(5) Special rule for master contract.–For purposes of this subsection, in the case of a master contract, the date taken into account with respect to any insured shall be the first date on which such insured is covered under such contract.

[Sec. 7702 A]

SEC. 7702 A. MODIFIED ENDOWMENT CONTRACT DEFINED.

[Sec. 7702 A(a)]

(a) GENERAL RULE.—For purposes of section 72, the term "modified endowment contract" means any contract meeting the requirements of section 7702—

(1) which—

(A) is entered into on or after June 21, 1988, and

(B) fails to meet the 7-pay test of subsection (b), or

(2) which is received in exchange for a contract described in paragraph (1).

[Sec. 7702A(b)]

(b) 7-PAY TEST.—For purposes of subsection (a), a contract fails to meet the 7-pay test of this subsection if the accumulated amount paid under the contract at any time during the 1st 7 contract years exceeds the sum of the net level premiums which would have been paid on or before such time if the contract provided for paid-up future benefits after the payment of 7 level annual premiums.

[Sec. 7702A(c)]

(c) COMPUTATIONAL RULES.—

(1) IN GENERAL.—Except as provided in this subsection, the determination under subsection (b) of the 7 level annual premiums shall be made—

(A) as of the time the contract is issued, and

160

(B) by applying the rules of section 7702(b)(2) and of section 7702(e) (other than paragraph (2)(C) thereof), except that the death benefit provided for the 1st contract year shall be deemed to be provided until the maturity date without regard to any scheduled reduction after the 1st 7 contract years.

(2) REDUCTION IN BENEFITS DURING 1ST 7 YEARS.—

APPENDIX G

TYPICAL TIMELINE FOR BOLI IMPLEMENTATION
(FROM DATE OF DECISION)

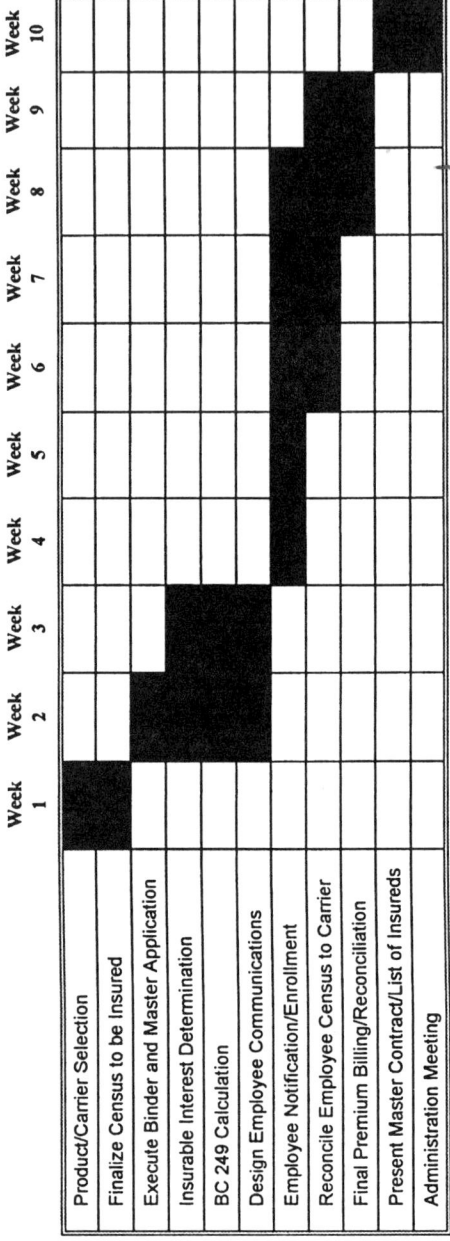

	Week 1	Week 2	Week 3	Week 4	Week 5	Week 6	Week 7	Week 8	Week 9	Week 10
Product/Carrier Selection	■									
Finalize Census to be Insured	■									
Execute Binder and Master Application		■								
Insurable Interest Determination		■	■							
BC 249 Calculation			■							
Design Employee Communications			■	■						
Employee Notification/Enrollment					■	■	■	■		
Reconcile Employee Census to Carrier							■	■	■	
Final Premium Billing/Reconciliation									■	
Present Master Contract/List of Insureds										■
Administration Meeting										■

APPENDIX H

[SAMPLE BANK]
EMPLOYEE LETTER REQUESTING CONSENT

January 1, 1996

Dear Employee:

[Sample Bank] is implementing a new Bank Owned Life Insurance Program. This program allows the corporation to attractively finance its employee benefit plan liabilities.

Under the plan, [Sample Bank] will purchase life insurance on a group of employees. [Sample Bank] will be the owner and the beneficiary of these policies.

There is no cost to you to participate, nor will your participation have any effect on your company-provided or personal life insurance programs, or other benefit plans.

This type of plan has been implemented by many of America's largest financial institutions as a means of helping to meet employee benefit plan liabilities. We believe it is appropriate for [Sample Bank] and its employees, and we fully support your participation.

Please return the attached form by [enrollment date], indicating your decision.

Please complete your card today and send it back to your Human Resources Department. If you have any questions, please call our consultants at 1-800-555-5555.

Sincerely,

[SAMPLE BANK]
EMPLOYEE LETTER NEGATIVE CONSENT

January 1, 1996

Dear Employee:

[Sample Bank] is implementing a new Bank Owned Life Insurance Program. This program allows the corporation to attractively finance its employee benefit plan liabilities.

Under the plan, the company will purchase life insurance on a group of employees. The company will be the owner and the beneficiary of these policies.

There is no cost to you to participate, nor will your participation have any effect on your company-provided or personal life insurance programs, or other benefit plans.

This type of plan has been implemented by many of America's largest companies as a means of helping to meet employee benefit plan liabilities. We believe it is appropriate for [Sample Bank] and its employees, and we fully support your participation.

If you do not wish to participate in the program, please contact the Human Resources Department by [enrollment date], indicating your decision. If we do not hear from you by that date, you will automatically be included in the program.

Sincerely,

[SAMPLE BANK]
BANK OWNED LIFE INSURANCE
INFORMATIONAL PAMPHLET

A Substantial Benefit for [Our Bank] and its Employees.

[Our Bank] is pleased to announce a new Bank Owned Life Insurance Plan. This plan has benefits for both [Our Bank] and our employees. Bank Owned Life Insurance (BOLI) is an investment for the company that relies on the support and participation of our employees. This program will provide:

- [Our Bank] with an additional, cost-effective source of funds that will help finance [Our Bank's business needs, including our employee benefits programs.
- [Our Bank] with a cash benefit upon your death, although under the BOLI program, the longer you live, the greater the financial benefit to [Our Bank].

This partnering with our employees provides another way for [Our Bank] to reduce costs and improve profitability. And as a result, you may receive an additional indirect benefit because as [Our Bank's] profitability improves, the annual percentage of your salary that the company contributes to your Retirement Savings and Profit Sharing Plan account also increases.

Thank you in advance for your participation in this very important program.

Sincerely,

How do I participate?

To participate in the plan, please return the enclosed enrollment form to _____, by [enrollment date].

How will participation affect my taxes?

There is no effect on your personal taxes.

Will I need to have a health examination?

No, all you do is fill out the form.

Will this program affect my group term life insurance coverage provided through [Our Bank] or any other personal life insurance?

No, this coverage does not have an impact on any other life insurance or company-provided benefits you may have.

Is my participation important?

Yes. [Our Bank]'s objective is 100 percent participation because the greater the participation, the greater the financial benefit to the company in its efforts to reduce costs and improve profitability.

What happens if I don't participate?

[Our Bank] will not purchase a life insurance contract on your life.

Who will record my participation?

The Plan Administrator will maintain a record of your participation.

How does the insurance program work?

[Our Bank] will purchase a life insurance policy on you. The amount of insurance is directly related to [Our Bank]'s employee benefit plan expenses. [Our Bank] will pay the premium. We will be the owner of the policy, and the beneficiary of the policy proceeds.

Is this program unique to [Our Bank]?

No, several large banks, including KeyCorp, First Bank System, Banc One, National City Bank and many others, have introduced similar programs over the past few years.

What will [Our Bank] do with the money it receives from the Insurance company?

All proceeds become part of company assets and will be used for corporate financing, including employee benefit programs.

Through which company is the insurance being purchased?

[Insurance carrier], one of the financially strongest insurance companies in North America.

Can the bank cancel the program at any time?

Yes.

Whom do I call for more information?

Call a member of the Benefit Coordination Team at 1-800- 555-5555 or your local human resources representative.

APPENDIX I

[SAMPLE BANK]
BANK OWNED LIFE INSURANCE CONSENT CARD

Please Print:

Last Name	First Name	Social Security No.	Date of Birth	Sex

Please Check One

❑ YES

Yes, I agree to participate in the [Our Bank] Bank Owned Life Insurance Program. I agree and understand that [Our Bank] will have all the rights of ownership, will pay all the premiums, and will be the beneficiary of the policy. I understand the reason for this insurance. I have received a letter from the Bank informing me that life insurance will be placed on my life and I agree to this insurance. I have been actively at work at [Our Bank] for the past 90 days, and have not missed five (5) consecutive days due to illness or injury.

❑ NO

No, I do not want to participate in this insurance program.

If you checked yes above, please complete the following:

Have you smoked cigarettes in the past 12 months?

❑ Yes   ❑ No   *(Check one)*

Signature Required:

_____

Signature   Date

GLOSSARY

Accredited Investor: as defined in Rule 502 of Regulation D, is any institution or individual meeting minimum net worth requirements for the purchase of securities qualifying under the Regulation D registration exemption. An accredited investor is generally accepted to be one who:
- has a net worth of $1 million or more; or
- has had an annual income of $200,000 or more in each of the two most recent years (or $300,000 jointly with a spouse) and who has a reasonable expectation of reaching the same income level in the current year.

Accumulation Account: is another term for cash value, such as found within a whole life policy. However, the accumulation account of a Universal Life policy can have a negative balance, unlike the cash value account.

ACE (Adjusted Current Earnings): is an adjustment intended to reflect a corporation's pre-tax net book income as measured for financial accounting purposes. Its purpose is to ensure that a corporation which reports a profit to the public or its shareholders reports that profit to the IRS as well. To calculate ACE, the corporation begins with AMTI, adds earnings and profits (such as income on a life insurance policy and receipt of key person insurance death proceeds), then subtracts certain deductible earnings (such as certain dividend income deductions). IRC Sec. 56(g). The corporation then recalculates depreciation once again according to specified methods to arrive at the final ACE adjustment. IRC Sec. 56(g)(4)(A). (TF-p.668)

AMT (Alternative Minimum Tax): for tax years beginning in 1990 and thereafter, corporations must calculate an Adjusted Current Earnings (ACE) amount and an Alternative Minimum Taxable Income (AMTI) amount. If the ACE exceeds the AMTI amount, then 75% of the ACE amount is added to the AMTI amount. Conversely, if the AMTI exceeds ACE, a reduction in the AMTI of 75% of the difference is permitted but this reduction cannot exceed the aggregate amount by which AMTI has been increased in prior tax years as a result of the ACE preference less the aggregate reductions allowed as a result of the preference for prior years.

AMTI (Alternative Minimum Taxable Income): (IRC Sec. 55(b)(2)) is regular taxable income determined with some adjustments and increased by certain tax preferences such as accelerated depreciation versus straight line, percentage of completion method over long-term contracts, no installment sale treatment of inventory, certified pollution control facilities depreciated under an alternative depreciation system, and mining exploration and development costs amortized over ten years (IRC Sec. 55(a)).

Basis Point (bp): 1 basis point is equal to 1/100 of 1 percent of yield. There are 100 basis points in 1 percentage point. For example, a yield that changes from 5.50 to 5.75 has moved up by 25 basis points.

BC 249 (OCC Banking Circular 249): was issued in 1991 with FASB Technical Bulletin 85-4 to define the purchase of life insurance by banks for the use of funding employee benefits and not for investment purposes. It addresses the legal and accounting guidelines in which banks may purchase life insurance.

Beneficiary: designation by the owner of a life insurance policy indicating to whom the proceeds are to be paid upon the insured's death or when an endowment matures. Anyone can be named a beneficiary (relative, non-relative, pet, charity, corporation, trustee, partnership).

Benefit Liabilities: the present and future costs incurred or to be incurred by a corporation associated with its employee benefit plans.

Binder Agreement: one of several closing documents, a binder is executed by the insurance carrier and a corporate purchaser in order to outline the terms for accepting a premium deposit prior to policy issue. In general, it establishes the policy date and coverage amounts prior to policy issue, has a fixed duration, and allows a provision for a deposit refund.

BOLI (Bank Owned Life Insurance): The bank purchases life insurance on its employees in order to finance employee benefit costs and to earn a tax-free yield on its investment. The amount of the purchase is based upon the expected total cost of the benefit plans during and after each employee's working lifetime for that bank. The amount of the BOLI purchased is such that it produces sufficient present value gains to equal (but which may not exceed) the present value cost of the total liabilities. The end result is that BOLI creates an immediate increase in net income and earnings per share.

Capital Adequacy Ratios: help define the structure of a bank's balance sheet in terms of risk-based capital values. These ratios give a picture of how the bank's assets are allocated among different investments. See Appendix C.

Carrier Risk: the risk associated with a change (drop) in an insurance carrier's credit rating.

Cash Value (Cash Surrender Value): money the policy owner is entitled to receive from the insurance company upon surrendering a life insurance policy with cash value. The sum is the cash value stated in the policy minus a surrender charge and any outstanding loans and interest thereon.

Cash Value Corridor Test: one of two tests applied to life insurance contracts under IRC Section 7702. A contract falls within this test if the death benefit payable under the contract at any time is at least equal to an applicable percentage of the cash surrender value. The test is in table form; see Appendix F.

Ceiling Rate (Cap): is a pre-determined maximum yield on the investment. In particular, it is the top side of the buyer's potential return of the PEP life insurance product.

Census: is a demographic snapshot of eligible employees to be used in calculating who will be insured and who will not be insured. Such characteristics of the census include the total number of employees of the corporation, the average age of the employee group, sex, and the number of officers or other eligible group. Also included in the census is benefit cost information such as post-retirement medical, life insurance, deferred compensation plans, and qualified retirement plans 401(k) matching contributions, defined benefit plans etc. The census is also used to determine the amount of insurable interest the corporation has on those employees.

Chassis: refers to the basic skeletal structure of an insurance product. Examples might be interest sensitive policies, universal policies, or variable policies.

COLI (Corporate Owned Life Insurance): insurance purchased by a corporation on the life of the employee, paid for by the company, with the company as the beneficiary. This insurance vehicle has been used to fund post-retirement employee plans, in which the cash values are listed as assets on the company's balance sheet.

Commissioners Standard Ordinary Mortality Table (CSO): table used in calculating minimum nonforfeiture values and policy reserves for ordinary life insurance policies. These tables, which give minimum values that must be guaranteed to policy owners as approved by the National Association of Insurance Commissioners (NAIC), depict the number of people dying each year out of the original population, not as individuals, but in age groups. The 1980 CSO Table is based on the mortality of Americans evaluated with a physical examination process in 1980.

Consent: compliance or approval of what is to be done or proposed by another. In the case of Bank Owned Life Insurance, consent is the approval by the employees of the purchase of the life insurance by the bank. Consent requirements are determined by state insurance laws and will depend upon the state in which the bank (owner of the policy) is located. The consent laws vary from state to state in one of the following four types:

Positive Consent—the employee must approve the purchase by signing a consent card. He/she has made a positive effort to agree to the purchase.

Negative Consent—also called "implied consent," uses the assumption that the employee approves the purchase unless there is a negative response objecting to the purchase given by the employee within a certain time period, usually 30 days.

Notification Only—requires that the purchaser of the policy simply notify the employee of the future purchase of life insurance on his/her life; positive or negative consent is not required in that state.

No Consent—consent is not required in any way; the bank has the right to purchase life insurance on the employee without consent or notification by the employee. The employee would be unaware of the purchase.

Crediting Rate: is the yield credited to the policy owner based upon cash value buildup in the policy.

Death Benefit: amount payable, as stated in a life insurance policy, upon the death of the insured. This is the face value of the policy plus any riders, less any outstanding loans and the interest accrued thereon.

Disintermediation Risk: flow of funds out of one financial instrument, whose interest rates are low, into another financial instrument, whose interest rates are higher. In the early 1980s, insurance companies experienced disintermediation as whole life polices were surrendered for their cash values and these sums were then transferred to higher interest-paying noninsurance products. Because of this situation, interest sensitive policies were developed by insurance companies.

Dividend: sum returned to a policy owner by an insurance company under a participation policy. Dividends are not deemed as taxable distributions, as the Internal Revenue Service interprets them as a refund of a portion of the premium paid. There are several ways in which the policy owner may use dividends.

Employee Benefit Plans: provision by an employer for the economic and social welfare of employees. Generally include: (1) pension plans for retirement; (2) group life insurance for death; (3) group health insurance for illness and accident; (4) group disability income insurance for the loss of income due to illness and accident; and (5) accidental death and dismemberment. Dental insurance, eyeglass insurance, and legal expense insurance may be included. These plans are established for the reasons of morale, to reduce turnover, and for tax benefits (contributions are usually deductible as business expenses to employers and not currently taxable income to employees).

Enrollment Timeline: a schedule of steps necessary to implement a COLI/BOLI life insurance program. Upon a positive decision to purchase, it begins with product/carrier selection and moves through various steps to the closing that consists of premium payment collection and a final administration meeting. The timelines for COLI and

BOLI will consist of the same steps, yet they may vary in overall length due to the nature of the products.

ERISA (Employee Retirement Income Security Act of 1974): law that established rules and regulations to govern private pension plans, including vesting requirements, funding mechanisms, and general plan design and descriptions.

Excess Interest: amount credited by carrier to policy values over and above guaranteed interest. Derived from carrier's investment profits.

FAS 106 (Statements of Standards): requires a corporation to accrue for the cost of post-retirement benefits other than pensions.

FAS 109 (Statements of Standards): underlies the accounting for income taxes and notes that if the difference of cash surrender value over premiums paid is not temporary, (as when the policy is to be held until death of the insured), policy income is free of tax.

FASB 85-4 (Technical Bulletin): is the primary accounting guide for recording the cash surrender value method of a life insurance policy. It explains how under this method, the premium payments are expensed and cash surrender values increases are reported as income.

FDIC (Federal Deposit Insurance Corporation): independent federal agency, established in 1933, that insures deposits up to $100,000 in member banks. It has its own reserves and can borrow from the U.S. Treasury, and sometimes acts to prevent bank failures, for instance, by facilitating bank mergers.

Federal Reserve Board: a seven-member group appointed by the president (subject to approval by Congress) to oversee operations of the Federal Reserve System.

Federal Reserve System (FED): system established by the Federal Reserve Act of 1913 to regulate the U.S. monetary and banking system. The Federal Reserve System is comprised of 12 regional Federal Reserve Banks, their 25 branches, and all national and state banks that are part of the system. National banks are stockholders of the Federal Reserve Bank in their Region. The Federal Reserve System's main functions are to regulate the national money supply, set reserve requirements for member banks, supervise the printing of currency at the mint, act as clearinghouse for the transfer of funds throughout the banking system, and examine member banks to make sure they meet various Federal Reserve System regulations.

Floor Rate: a predetermined, guaranteed minimum yield on the investment. In particular, it is the bottom side of the buyer's potential return of the PEP life insurance product.

Front-End Load: a sales charge paid with the first premium that is in addition to the pure cost of insurance. It reflects agent commissions, premium taxes and administrative costs associated with putting business on an insurance company's books, and contingencies.

GAAP (Generally Accepted Accounting Principles): type of accounting method, in life insurance, designed to match revenues and expenses of an insurer according to principles designed by the Financial Accounting Standards Board (FASB) and the Audit Guide for Stock Life Insurance Companies published by the American Institute of CPAs. For example, under GAAP, acquisition expenses (costs of placing insurance on a company's books such as administrative expenses and agent commissions) are recognized in the same proportion that premium income is recognized over the premium paying period, with losses subtracted from premium and investment income as they occur.

General Account Products: are life insurance products that are structured with carrier investments that are found or held within the carrier's general account (as opposed to a separate account). They are fixed rate products with yields that are reset annually based upon the investments within the general account. Because this account is the main portfolio account of the carrier, it is what helps determine the carrier's credit rating.

Guaranteed Issue: the right to purchase insurance without physical examination; the present and past physical condition of the applicant are not considered. Normally, the insurance carrier will issue coverage on all employees designated who have been actively at work for the past 90 days without interruption. The insurance carrier uses mortality tables to price the impact of issuing the coverage based on the law of large numbers.

Guideline Single Premium Test: is the premium necessary to fund future benefits under the contract, determined at the time the contract is issued. This test is one of two tests used to define a life insurance contract and can be found in IRC 7702.

Insurable Interest: expectation of a monetary loss that can be covered by insurance.

Insurance: mechanism for contractually shifting burdens of a number of pure risks by pooling them.

Investment: A vehicle for funds, expected to maintain or increase its value and/or generate positive returns.

Investment Company Act of 1940: act that regulates the variable dollar insurance products (equity related) sold by insurance companies. The act includes regulations that stipulate: (1) the variable dollar insurance products must be funded through a separate account (segregated from the other investment accounts of the insurance company); (2) benefits and cash values must vary in tandem with the investment returns of this separate account; (3) mortality and expense fluctuations (above the maximum chargeable stipulated in the policy) must be borne by the insurance company; (4) maximum sales load; and (5) periodic financial reports must be sent to the policy owner.

Investment Grade Bonds: or "Bank Grade Bonds" are bonds that have a high credit rating and a high probability to repay their debt obligation upon maturity. For example, Standard & Poor's investment grade bonds are rated BBB or higher. Bonds below this rating are considered non-investment grade or "Speculative" bonds.

IRC Section 1035a: also called a "1035 Exchange," allows a policyholder a tax-free exchange of a life insurance policy for another policy. The exchange may be within the existing company or to an outside company. For example, if the credit rating of a carrier drops the policyholder may switch to policy over to a more stable carrier. They may also exchange the policy from a fixed contract to a variable contract. In any case, the exchange of the policy must be on the life of the same insured.

IRC Section 264(c): defines the owner's right of tax deductibility of interest paid due to indebtedness taken on the purchase of single and non-single premium life insurance policies.

IRC Section 7702: is the definition of a life insurance contract. It defines the effects of taxation upon such issues as policy distributions, annuities, cash value increases, death proceeds, and policy loans. In order for a contract to be classified as a life insurance contract, it must meet one of two alternative tests; (1) the cash value accumulation test, (2) the guideline premium and cash value corridor test. See Appendix F.

IRS (Internal Revenue Service): agency of the federal government that is responsible for the administration and collection of federal income taxes. The IRS prints and distributes tax forms and audits tax returns. It is part of the Department of the Treasury.

Legal Lending Limits: statutory limit applied to banks/financial institutions regarding loans made to a single entity. This amount is a function of stockholder equity.

Leveraged COLI (Leveraged Corporate Owned Life Insurance): the policy holder borrows against the cash value of the policy and deducts a portion of the interest expense. Narrowly viewed, these borrowings minimize net cash investment in the policy while the cash values continue to grow at the declared rate of interest. The result is an increased or leveraged net yield to the policy. See the definition of COLI.

M & E Charge: the mortality and expense charge paid to the issuing carrier which includes the non-investment cost of an insurance contract.

MEC (Modified Endowment Contract): a type of contract that meets the requirements of Code section 7702, was entered into on or after June 21, 1988, and fails to meet the seven pay test. Distributions from MECs are subject to taxation rules that differ from the rules governing the taxation of distributions from life insurance policies that are not MECs. Note that most BOLI transactions are MECs.

Mortality Charge: the pure cost of life insurance death benefit within a policy. It represents a cost to the purchaser and an income item to the carrier. Mortality charges retained by the carrier are used to pay claims.

Mutual Insurance Company: company owned by its policy owners; no stock is available for purchase on the stock exchanges.

NASD (National Association of Securities Dealers): organization of brokers and securities dealers in the over-the-counter market operation under the auspices of the

Securities and Exchange Commission (SEC). Its purpose is to enforce, on a self-regulation basis, the rules of the SEC which are designed to protect investors against fraud and market manipulation of stocks. Insurance agents selling variable life insurance, variable annuities and mutual funds are required to be licensed by the NASD.

Net Coverage Amount: is the dollar face amount or death benefit amount of the life insurance policy less any outstanding loans or interest expense.

Nonforfeiture Values: are benefits of an individual whole life insurance policy that cannot be given up by the carrier. The policy owner has the right to choose from four different options: (1) to relinquish the policy for its cash surrender value; (2) to take reduced paid-up insurance; (3) to take extended term insurance; (4) to use the loan value to borrow against the policy.

Non-MEC: an insurance contract that is not a Modified Endowment Contract. It is any insurance contract where the majority of premiums are made after the first of three years.

Nonqualified: benefit plans that are not approved by the IRS for tax breaks and which do not have to follow ERISA regulations. With a nonqualified plan, the same benefit plans do not have to be offered to all employees; employees can be chosen by the corporation depending upon who they want to give the benefit to. An example would be a nonqualified deferred income plan.

Nonaccredited Investor: is an investor not meeting the net worth requirements of Regulation D. Nonaccredited investors are counted for purposes of the 35-investor limitation under Rules 505 and 506 of Regulation D.

OCC (Office of the Comptroller of the Currency): was created as a result of the National Currency Act of 1863 and the National Banking Act of 1964. The OCC is the prime regulator for all U.S. nationally chartered banks and is the organization that performs examinations and rulings on the national banks.

OTS (Office of Thrift Supervision): was created by Congress in 1989 to assume most of the regulatory and supervisory powers of the Federal Home Loan Bank Board, which Congress disbanded that year. The OTS charters federal savings and loan associations and federal savings banks. However, these institutions are examined by the FDIC, which administers the insurance fund for S & Ls. The OTS is responsible for issuing regulations that govern the activities of S & Ls and S & L holding companies.

Paid Up Insurance: life insurance policy under which all premiums have already been paid, with no further premium payment due, such as a limited or single payment life insurance policy.

Participation Rate: the yield on the PEP life insurance product that is based upon a certain amount of investment participation in the S&P 500 index. This rate will lie somewhere between the guaranteed floor rate and the maximum ceiling rate of the product.

Pecuniary: consisting of money, that which can be valued in money. A pecuniary loss is a loss of money or one that can be translated in terms of money.

Pension Plan (Benefits): retirement program to provide employees (and often, spouses) with a monthly income payment for the rest of their lives. To qualify, an employee must have met minimum age and service requirements. Benefit formulas can be either the defined contribution pension (money purchase plan) or the defined benefit plan. The Employee Retirement Security Act of 1974 (ERISA) requires a pension plan to provide an income for the rest of a retired employee's life, and at least 50% of that amount to the surviving spouse of a retired employee for the rest of his/her life, unless the spouse waives this right in writing. Death and disability benefits are also provided by most pension plans. The Tax Reform Act of 1986 has changed the vesting requirements. Funds for these plans can be generated under numerous pension plan funding instruments.

PEP: (Protected Equity Plan) is a hybrid form of BOLI incorporating the best features of both Annual Fixed Yield and Variable Yield insurance. It provides a guaranteed floor and a modified variable yield. The nature of this product involves investment participation in the S&P 500 index. The PEP yield is guaranteed to the greater of a percentage participation in the S&P 500 index annual increase with a set maximum ceiling yield and a minimum set floor yield. It offers the features of a high tax-free yield, a guaranteed minimum floor yield, guarantee of principal and liquidity. It is the first life insurance policy to receive Patent Pending protection.

Policy Date (Effective Date): date on which an insurance policy goes into force.

Policy Loan: In life insurance, a loan can be taken against the cash value of a life insurance policy at any time. The policyholder does not have to repay the loan until the policy matures or until the loan and any outstanding interest equals the cash value.

Policy Reserve (Prospective Reserve): amount designated as a future liability for life or health insurance to meet the difference between future benefits and future premiums.

Portfolio Product: an insurance product where the carrier places its funds in its general portfolio of investments and credits a yield to the policy based on its portfolio yield. The general portfolio consists of conservative investments that produce a fixed crediting yield where the investment control and risk is solely borne by the carrier. The policy yield is reset annually and has a guaranteed floor.

184

Premium: the rate that an insured is charged, reflecting his or her expectation of loss or risk. The insurance company will assume the risks of the insured in exchange for a premium payment. Premiums are calculated by combining expectation of loss and expense and profit loading.

Private Placement: is a technique used by insurance companies in the purchasing of debt obligations of corporations as a means to: (1) avoid the uncertainties of the market; (2) replace market negotiations with private negotiations; and (3) avoid SEC restrictions. (I-p.373) It is an offering that complies with Regulation D (Rule 505 and 506); generally speaking, the offer of an unregistered security to no more than 35 nonaccredited investors or to an unlimited number of accredited investors.

Proceeds: benefits payable under any insurance policy or annuity contract.

Protected Equity Plan: (PEP) is a hybrid form of BOLI incorporating the best features of both Annual Fixed Yield and Variable Yield insurance. It provides a guaranteed floor and a modified variable yield. The nature of this product involves for investment participation in the S&P 500 index. The PEP yield is guaranteed to the greater of a percentage participation in the S&P 500 index annual increase with a set maximum ceiling yield and a minimum set floor yield. It offers the features of a high tax-free yield, a guaranteed minimum floor yield, guarantee of principal, and liquidity. It is the first life insurance policy to receive Patent Pending protection.

Qualified: such as a "qualified pension benefit plan" that has been approved for certain tax breaks and follows the stringent set of ERISA guidelines. With a qualified plan, the same benefits must be offered to all employees.

RAP (Regulatory Accounting Principals): are guidelines set by bank regulators, particularly the Federal Reserve and OCC regulators, that are different from GAAP principals. RAP principals place limits or requirements on certain balance sheet items that banks must adhere to. These principals do not affect BOLI transactions.

Registered Product: a security (including variable insurance products) must be registered just as sales representatives and broker-dealers must be registered before they can offer or sell a security in a state. Under the guidelines of the Uniform Securities Act, no person can offer to sell any security in a state lawfully unless the: (1) security is registered under the Uniform Securities Act; (2) security is designated by the act as exempt from registration requirement; or (3) transaction is designated by the act as exempt from registration requirement. If a security is not exempt from the registration requirement, the security is called a *nonexempt security.*

Regulation D: the securities regulation that exempts small public offerings from registration (those valued at no more than $5 million worth of securities offered during a 12-month period).

Risk-Based Capital: is the definitional guidelines for bank held assets defined by the Federal Reserve, the OCC, and the FDIC. There are four classifications of bank assets calculated as a function of risk. The classifications begin with Tier 1 (least risky) through Tier 4 (most risky). Each tier is weighted based upon its riskiness so as to indicate on the bank's balance sheet how the assets are invested. See table in Appendix C.

SEC (Security Exchange Commission): Federal agency empowered to regulate and supervise the selling of securities, to prevent unfair practices on security exchanges and over-the-counter markets, and to maintain fair and orderly market for the investor.

Securities Act of 1933: landmark legislation passed by Congress providing the first regulation of the securities markets. The law, enforced by the Securities and Exchange Commission (SEC), requires registration of securities issues and disclosure of material information about the financial condition of the issuers. Variable annuity and variable life insurance policies have been determined to be securities under the terms of this law and are subject to regulation both by the SEC and by state insurance departments.

Securities Exchange Act of 1934: was enacted after the Securities Act of 1933, which regulates the primary issuance of securities. The Act of 1934 regulates the secondary trading of securities. The intent of this act is to maintain a fair and orderly market for the investing public. It seeks to attain this goal by regulating the securities exchanges and the over-the-counter markets. Commonly called the Exchange Act, it formed the Securities Exchange Commission and gave the Commission authority to oversee the secondary markets and to register and regulate the exchanges. It requires several other entities to register with the SEC, including exchange members and broker-dealers that trade securities OTC and on exchanges and individuals who effect securities trades with the public.

Separate Account Products: life insurance products that are structured with carrier investments that are not found or held within the carrier's general account. They are variable rate products that have fluctuating yields based upon the investments within the separate account. Because this account is "separate" from the main, general account of the carrier, it reduces what is called carrier risk for the buyer's behalf.

Seven Pay Test: applies to the test of a MEC. A policy will fail this test if the accumulated amount paid under the first seven years exceeds the sum net level premiums (the MEC level).

Single Premium: one premium payment is made and the policy is fully paid up with no further premiums required. Also, if all of the premiums are paid within four years from the date of purchase or on which an amount is deposited with the insurer for the future payment of premiums (of a substantial amount greater than 73 percent).

Split Dollar Life Insurance: is the most frequently used form of permanent life insurance as an executive compensation benefit. This type of plan splits a life insurance policy's premium obligation and policy benefit between two individuals or entities, usually employer and employee. The two parties share the premium costs while the policy is in effect, pursuant to a prearranged agreement. At the death of the insured or the termination of the agreement, the parties split the policy benefits or proceeds in accordance with their agreement.

Stochastic: a statistical term which describes a variable with values determined by chance (a random variable). In regression analysis, the dependent variable is stochastic if the model does not perfectly explain all observations.

Stock Insurance Company: business owned by stockholders, as contrasted to a mutual insurance company, which is owned by its policyholders. Earnings of a stock insurance company are paid in shareholder dividends. Many major life insurers are mutual companies whereas some leading property/casualty and multi-line insurers are stock insurance companies.

Stockholders' Equity: is a balance sheet item that includes the book value of ownership in the corporation. It includes capital stock, paid-in surplus and retained earnings. It is equal to the total assets minus the total liabilities of the corporation. It is also known as net worth.

Test A (of BC 249): the test that allows banks to purchase life insurance on "key employees" in the case of a loss of a key employee.

Test B (of BC 249): the test that allows banks to purchase life insurance on its employees to finance compensation agreements and benefit plan obligations. The calculations maybe performed on an aggregate or group basis as opposed to an individual basis.

Universal Life Insurance: adjustable life insurance under which: (1) premiums are flexible, not fixed; (2) protection is adjustable, not fixed; and (3) insurance company expenses and other charges are specifically disclosed to a purchaser. This policy is referred to as unbundled life insurance because its three basic elements (investment earnings, pure cost of protection, and company expenses) are separately identified both in the policy and in annual report to the policy owner.

Variable Life Insurance: investment-oriented life insurance policy that provides a return linked to an underlying portfolio of securities. The portfolio typically is a group of mutual funds established by the insurer as a separate account, with the policyholder given some investment discretion in choosing the mix of assets among, say, a common stock fund, a bond fund, and a money market fund. Variable life insurance offers fixed premiums and a minimum death benefit. The better the total return on the investment portfolio, the higher the death benefit or surrender value of the variable life policy.

Whole Life Insurance (Ordinary Life Insurance): policy that remains in full force and effect for life of the insured, with premium payments being made for the same period.

Withdrawal (Cash Withdrawal): removal of money from an individual life insurance policy or an employee benefit plan. A cash withdrawal from a life insurance policy reduces the death benefit by the amount of the withdrawal plus interest thereon. When a cash withdrawal is made from an employee benefit such as a pension plan, the employee usually forfeits all benefits purchased on the employee's behalf by the employer.

Yield: the rate of return on an investment.

BIBLIOGRAPHY

Dictionary of Business Terms, Barron's Educational Series, Inc., Hauppauge, NY, 1987

Dictionary of Insurance Terms, Third Edition, Barron's Educational Series, Inc., Hauppauge, NY, 1995

Money & Banking, Third Edition, American Bankers Association, Washington, D.C., 1993

McGill's Life Insurance, Edward G. Graves, The American College, Second Printing, Bryn Mawr, Pennsylvania, 1994

Tax Facts 1, 1994 Edition, The National Underwriter Company, Cincinnati, OH